PRIMATES

JIM OTTAVIANI & MARIS WICKS

PRIMATES

The Fearless Science of Jane Goodall, Dian Fossey, and Biruté Galdikas

First Second
New York

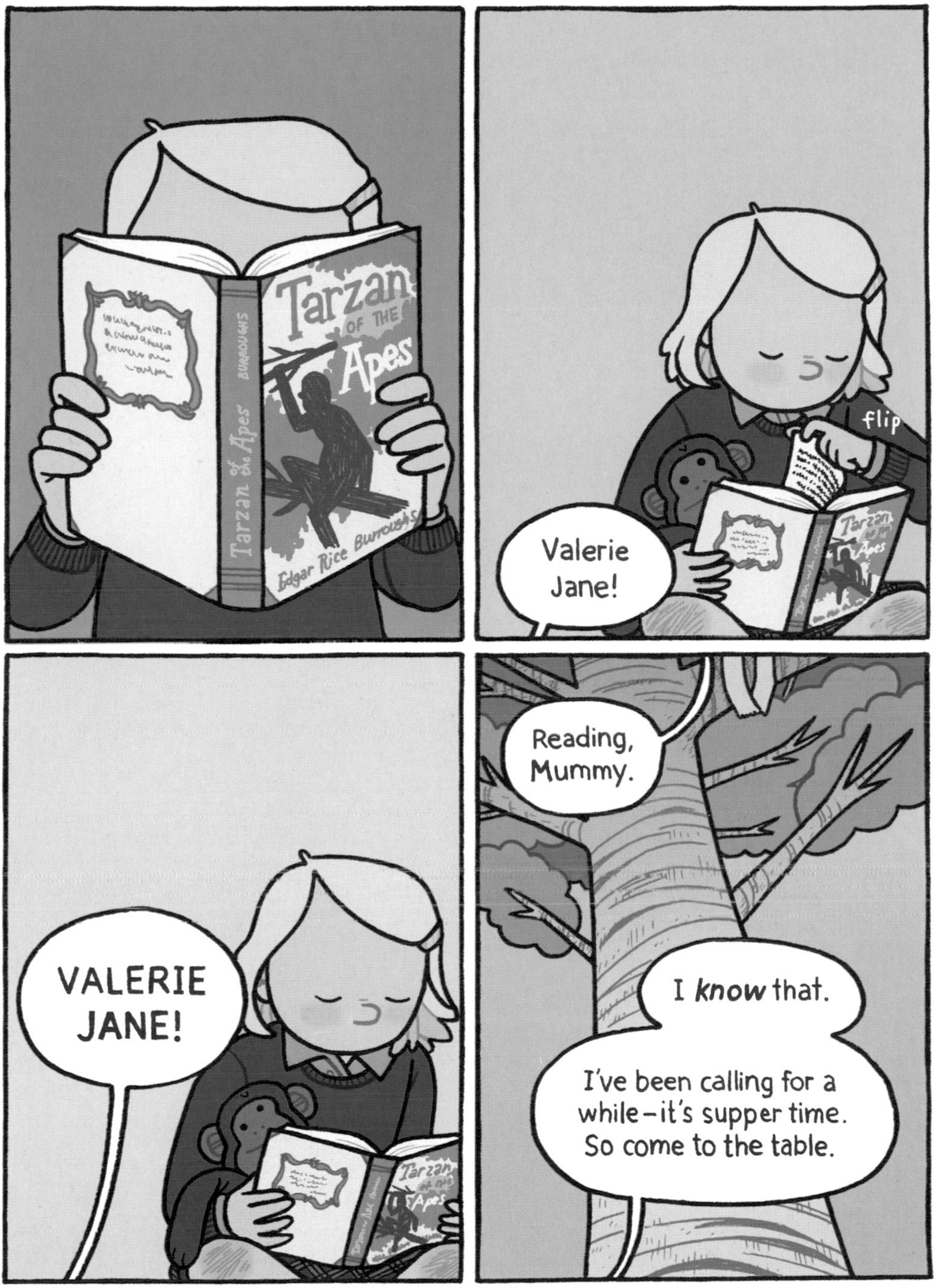
Tarzan OF THE Apes
Tarzan of the Apes
BURROUGHS
Edgar Rice Burroughs
flip
Valerie Jane!
VALERIE JANE!
Reading, Mummy.
I *know* that.
I've been calling for a while–it's supper time. So come to the table.

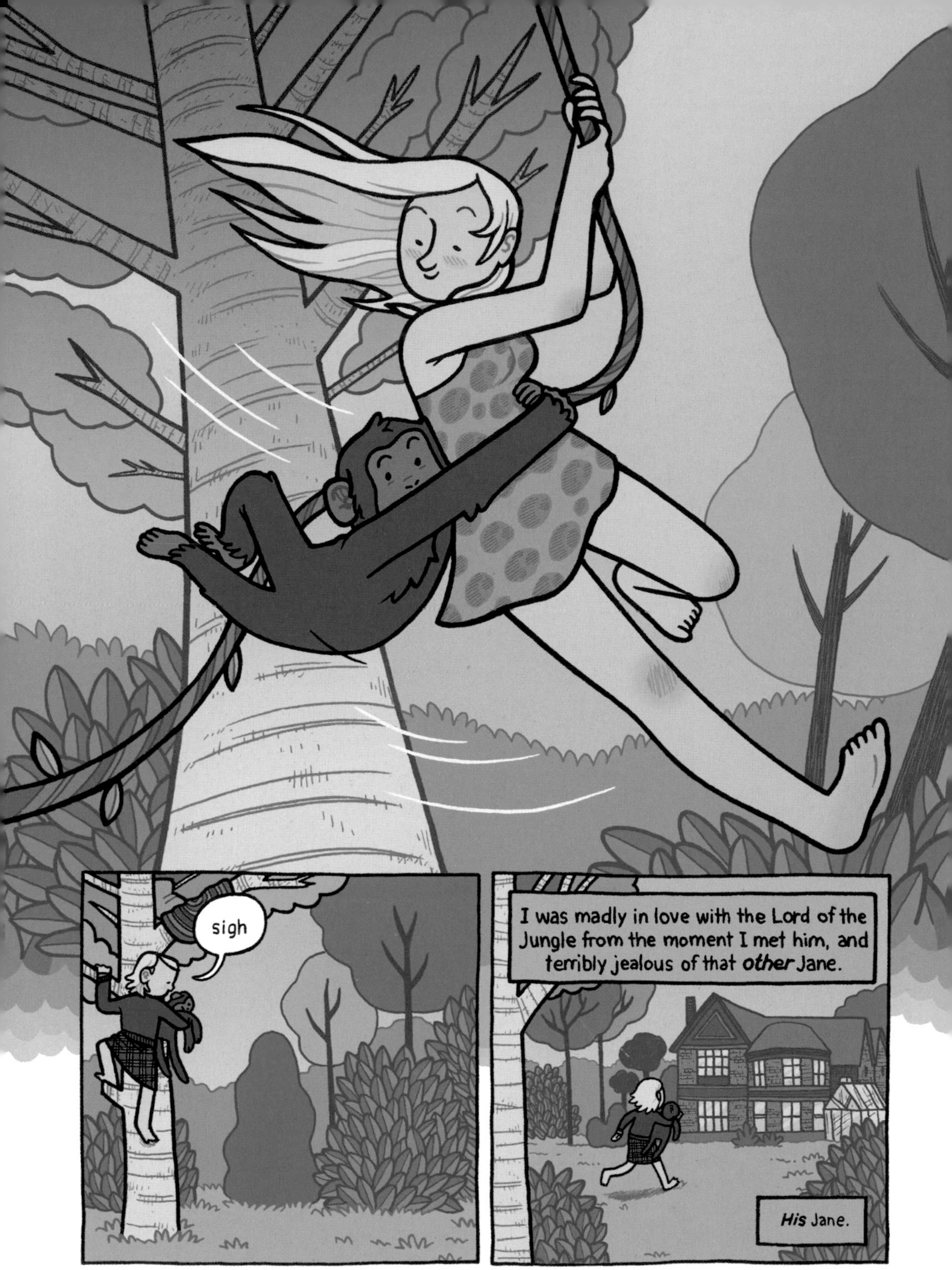
sigh
I was madly in love with the Lord of the Jungle from the moment I met him, and terribly jealous of that *other* Jane.
His Jane.

Part 1: But in my dreams, I did bigger things.

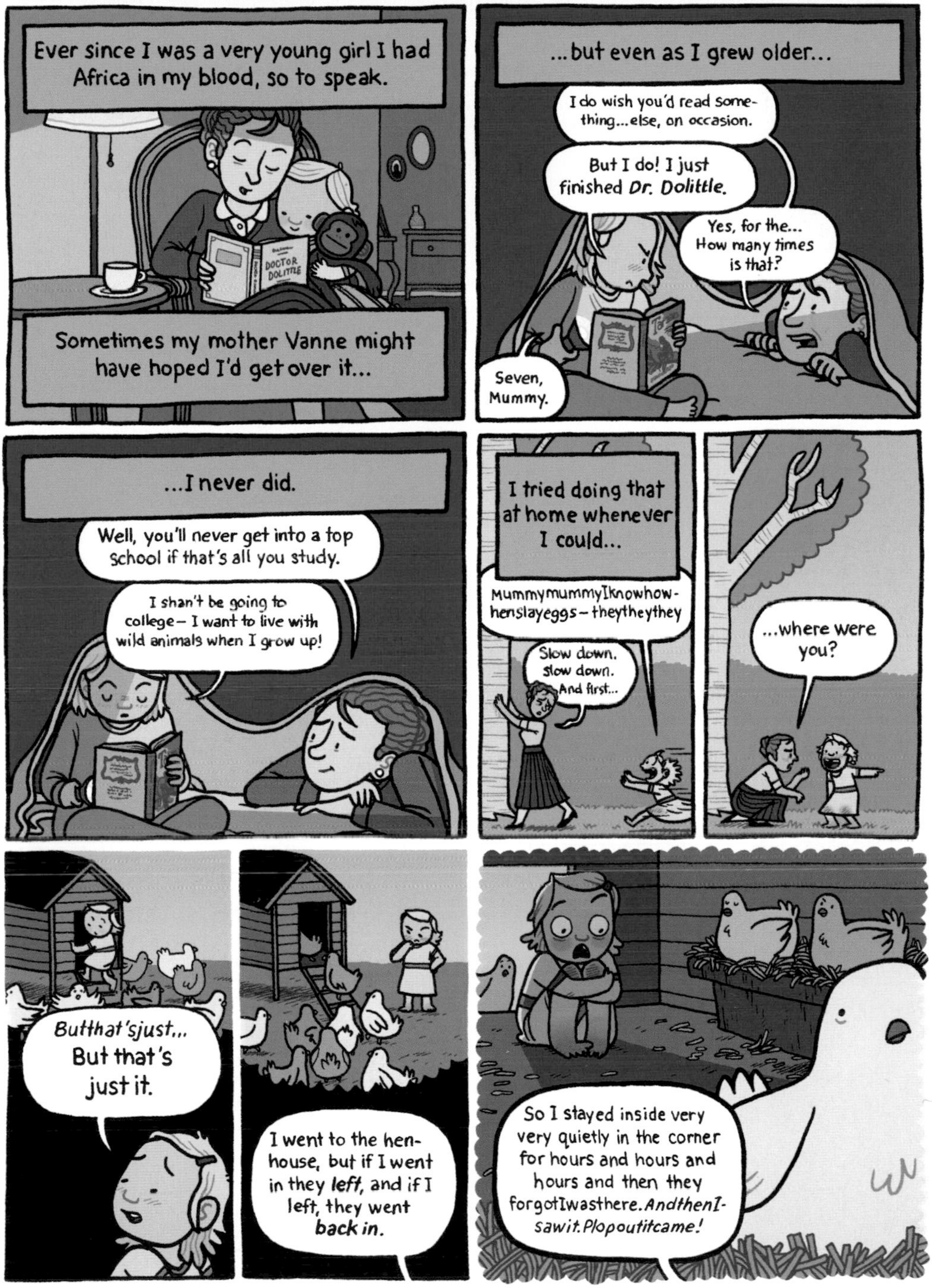
Ever since I was a very young girl I had Africa in my blood, so to speak.
DOCTOR DOLITTLE
Sometimes my mother Vanne might have hoped I'd get over it...
...but even as I grew older...
I do wish you'd read something...else, on occasion.
But I do! I just finished Dr. Dolittle.
Yes, for the... How many times is that?
Seven, Mummy.
...I never did.
Well, you'll never get into a top school if that's all you study.
I shan't be going to college– I want to live with wild animals when I grow up!
I tried doing that at home whenever I could...
MummymummyIknowhowhenslayeggs–theytheythey
Slow down. slow down. And first...
...where were you?
Butthat'sjust... But that's just it.
I went to the henhouse, but if I went in they *left*, and if I left, they went **back in**.
So I stayed inside very very quietly in the corner for hours and hours and hours and then they forgotIwasthere. *AndthenIsawit.Plopoutitcame!*

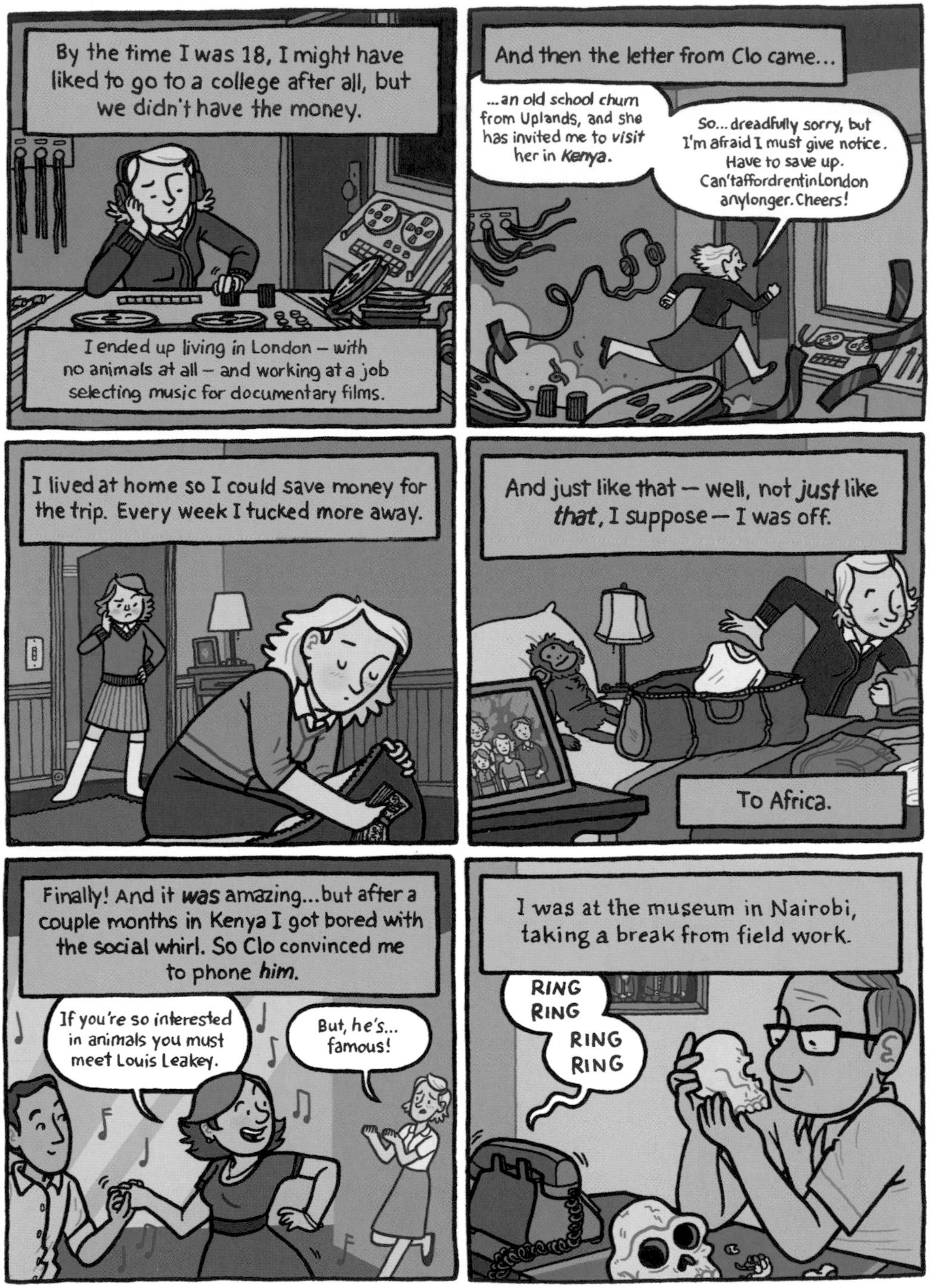
By the time I was 18, I might have liked to go to a college after all, but we didn't have the money.
I ended up living in London – with no animals at all – and working at a job selecting music for documentary films.
And then the letter from Clo came...
...an old school chum from Uplands, and she has invited me to *visit* her in *Kenya*.
So... dreadfully sorry, but I'm afraid I must give notice. Have to save up. Can'taffordrentinLondon anylonger. Cheers!
I lived at home so I could save money for the trip. Every week I tucked more away.
And just like that – well, not *just* like *that*, I suppose – I was off.
To Africa.
Finally! And it *was* amazing... but after a couple months in Kenya I got bored with the social whirl. So Clo convinced me to phone *him*.
If you're so interested in animals you must meet Louis Leakey.
But, he's... famous!
I was at the museum in Nairobi, taking a break from field work.
RING RING
RING RING

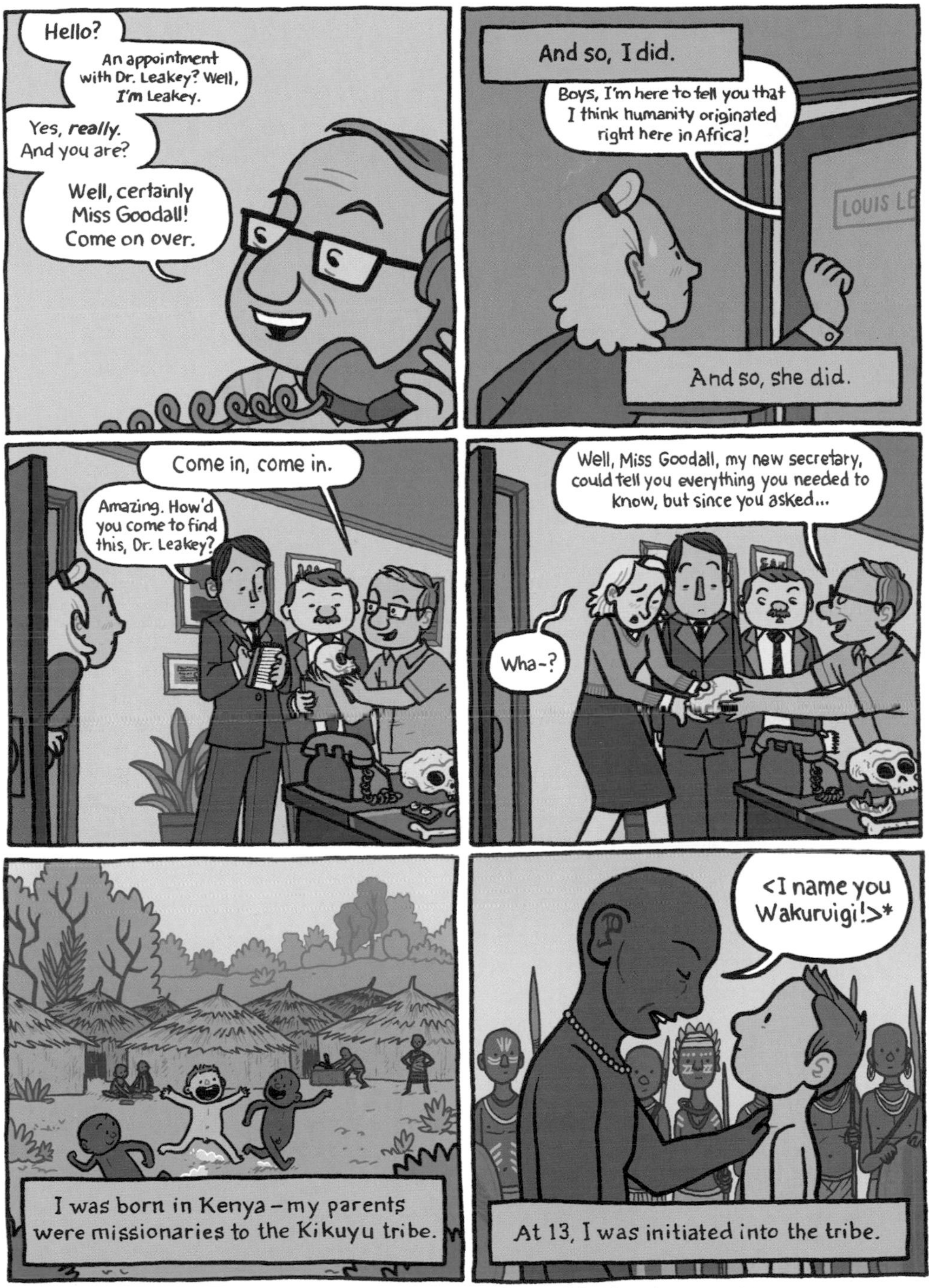
Hello?
An appointment with Dr. Leakey? Well, *I'm* Leakey.
Yes, *really.* And you are?
Well, certainly Miss Goodall! Come on over.
And so, I did.
Boys, I'm here to tell you that I think humanity originated right here in Africa!
LOUIS LE
And so, she did.
Come in, come in.
Amazing. How'd you come to find this, Dr. Leakey?
Well, Miss Goodall, my new secretary, could tell you everything you needed to know, but since you asked...
Wha-?
I was born in Kenya – my parents were missionaries to the Kikuyu tribe.
<I name you Wakuruigi!>*
At 13, I was initiated into the tribe.

*<translated from Kikuyu> – Wakuruigi means "Son of the Sparrow Hawk"

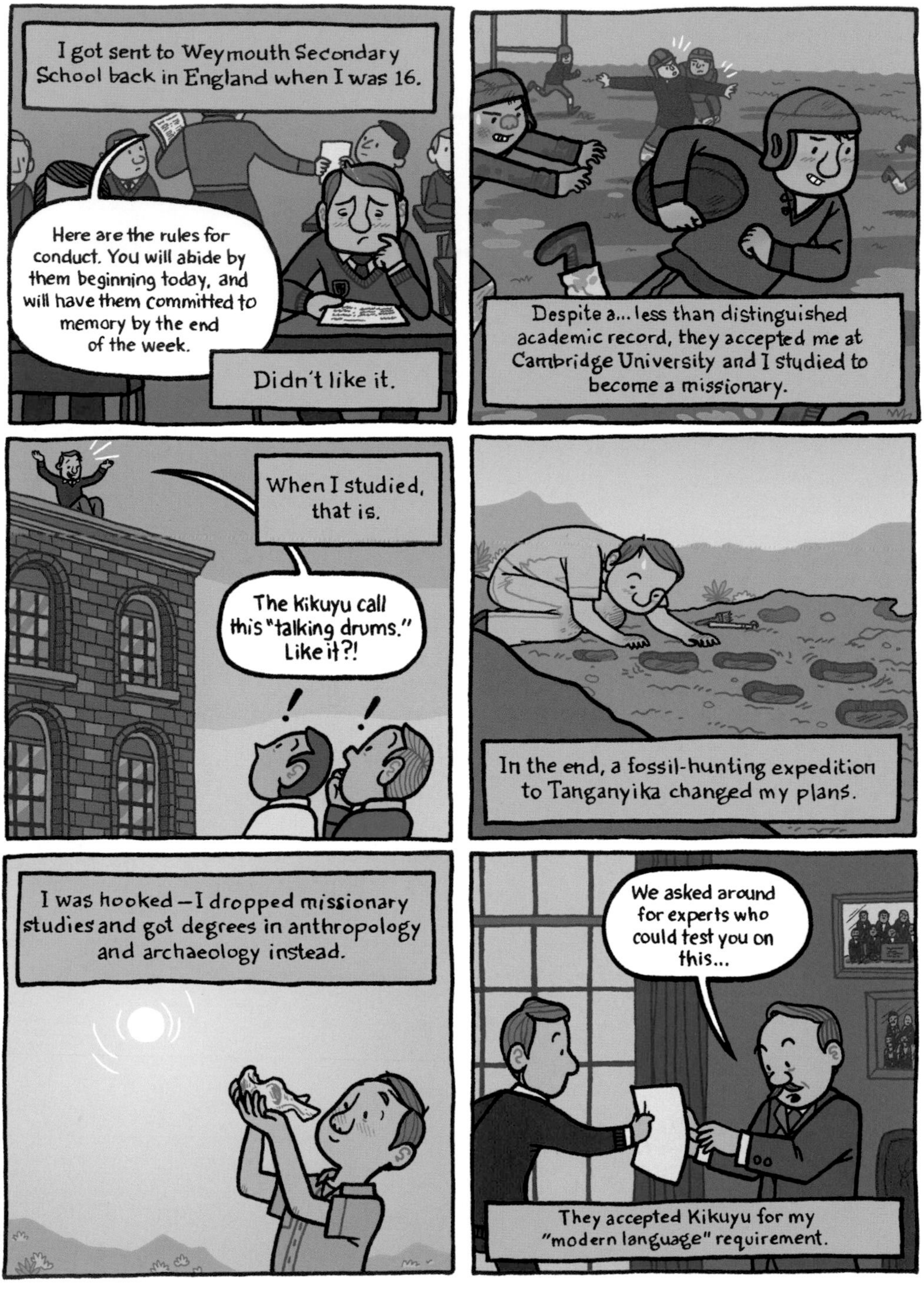
I got sent to Weymouth Secondary School back in England when I was 16.
Here are the rules for conduct. You will abide by them beginning today, and will have them committed to memory by the end of the week.
Didn't like it.
Despite a... less than distinguished academic record, they accepted me at Cambridge University and I studied to become a missionary.
When I studied, that is.
The Kikuyu call this "talking drums." Like it?!
!
!
In the end, a fossil-hunting expedition to Tanganyika changed my plans.
I was hooked—I dropped missionary studies and got degrees in anthropology and archaeology instead.
We asked around for experts who could test you on this...
They accepted Kikuyu for my "modern language" requirement.

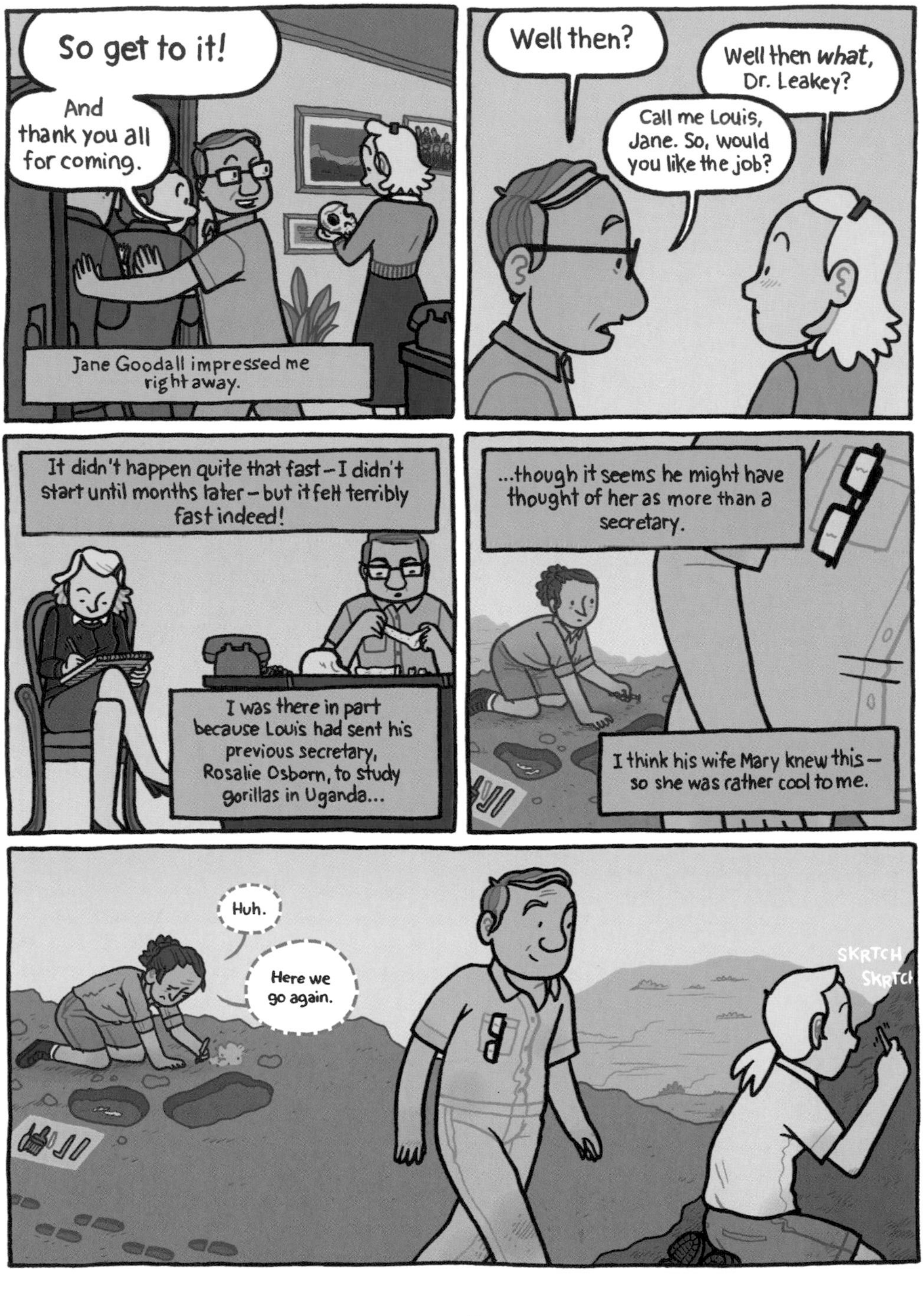
So get to it!
And thank you all for coming.
Jane Goodall impressed me right away.
Well then?
Well then *what*, Dr. Leakey?
Call me Louis, Jane. So, would you like the job?
It didn't happen quite that fast—I didn't start until months later—but it felt terribly fast indeed!
I was there in part because Louis had sent his previous secretary, Rosalie Osborn, to study gorillas in Uganda...
...though it seems he might have thought of her as more than a secretary.
I think his wife Mary knew this—so she was rather cool to me.
Huh.
Here we go again.
SKRTCH
SKRTCH

9

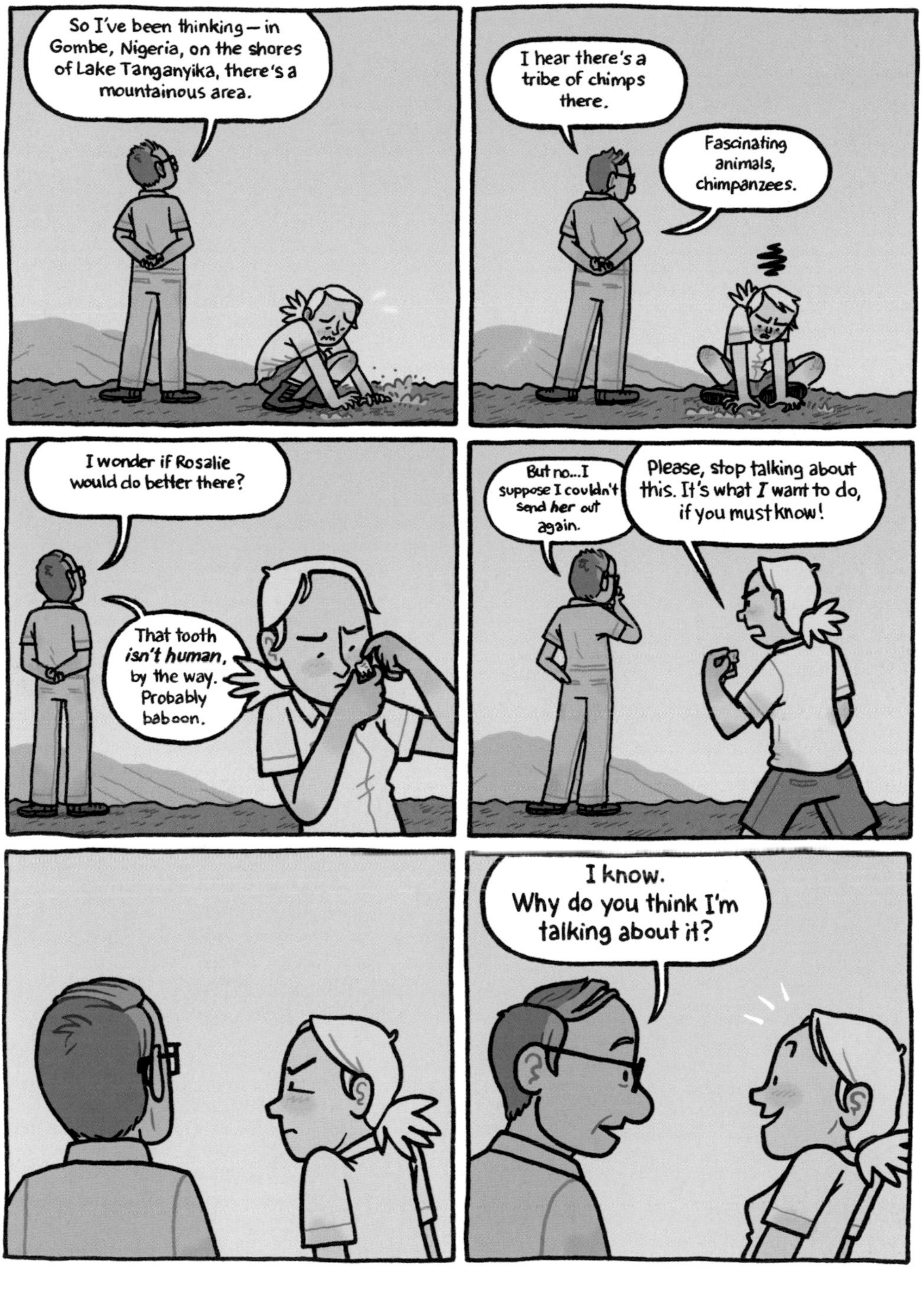
So I've been thinking — in Gombe, Nigeria, on the shores of Lake Tanganyika, there's a mountainous area.
I hear there's a tribe of chimps there.
Fascinating animals, chimpanzees.
I wonder if Rosalie would do better there?
That tooth *isn't human*, by the way. Probably baboon.
But no...I suppose I couldn't send *her* out again.
Please, stop talking about this. It's what *I* want to do, if you must know!
I know. Why do you think I'm talking about it?

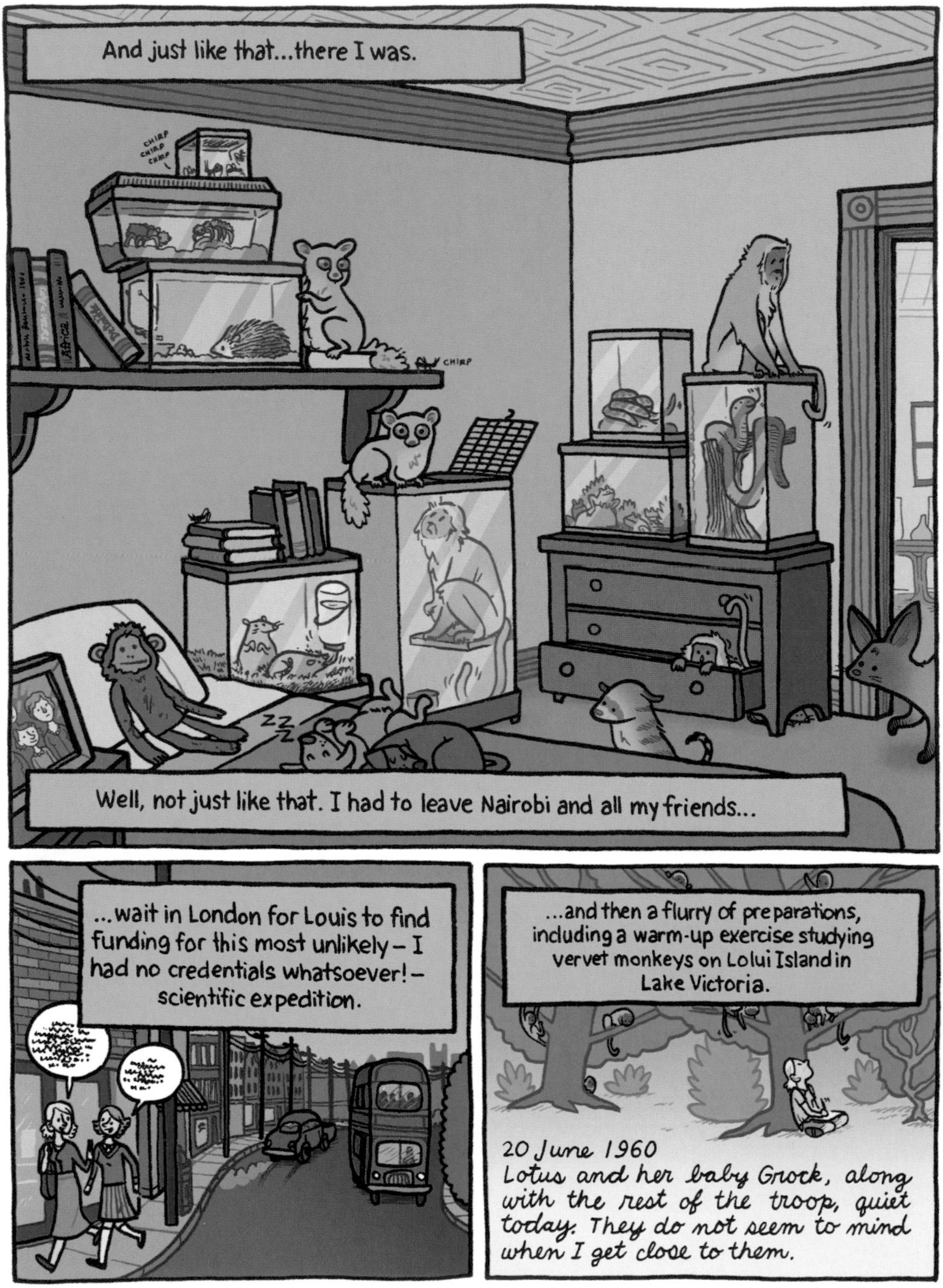
And just like that...there I was.
CHIRP CHIRP CHIRP
CHIRP
Well, not just like that. I had to leave Nairobi and all my friends...
...wait in London for Louis to find funding for this most unlikely – I had no credentials whatsoever! – scientific expedition.
...and then a flurry of preparations, including a warm-up exercise studying vervet monkeys on Lolui Island in Lake Victoria.
20 June 1960
Lotus and her baby Grock, along with the rest of the troop, quiet today. They do not seem to mind when I get close to them.

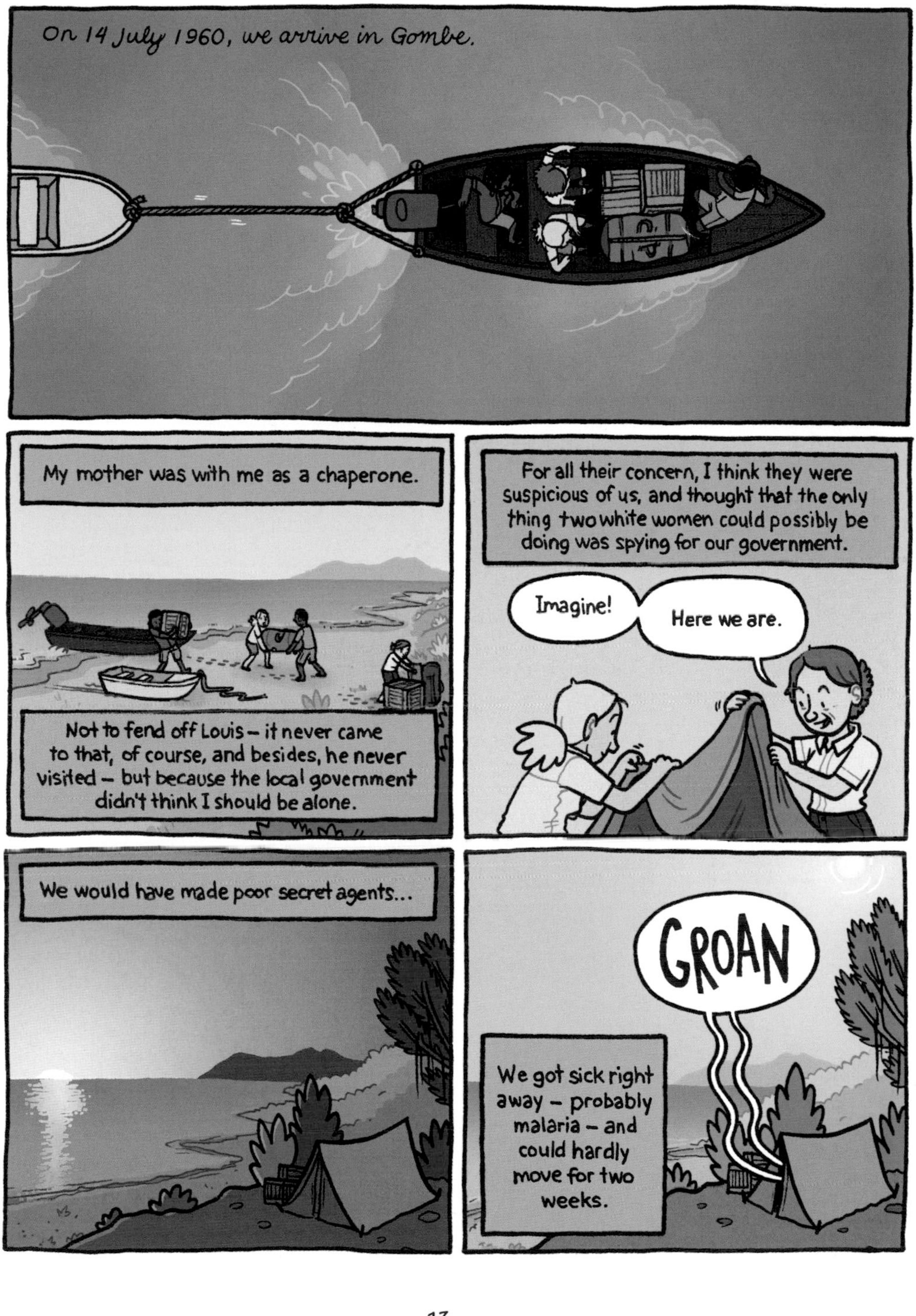
On 14 July 1960, we arrive in Gombe.
My mother was with me as a chaperone.
Not to fend off Louis – it never came to that, of course, and besides, he never visited – but because the local government didn't think I should be alone.
For all their concern, I think they were suspicious of us, and thought that the only thing two white women could possibly be doing was spying for our government.
Imagine!
Here we are.
We would have made poor secret agents...
GROAN
We got sick right away – probably malaria – and could hardly move for two weeks.

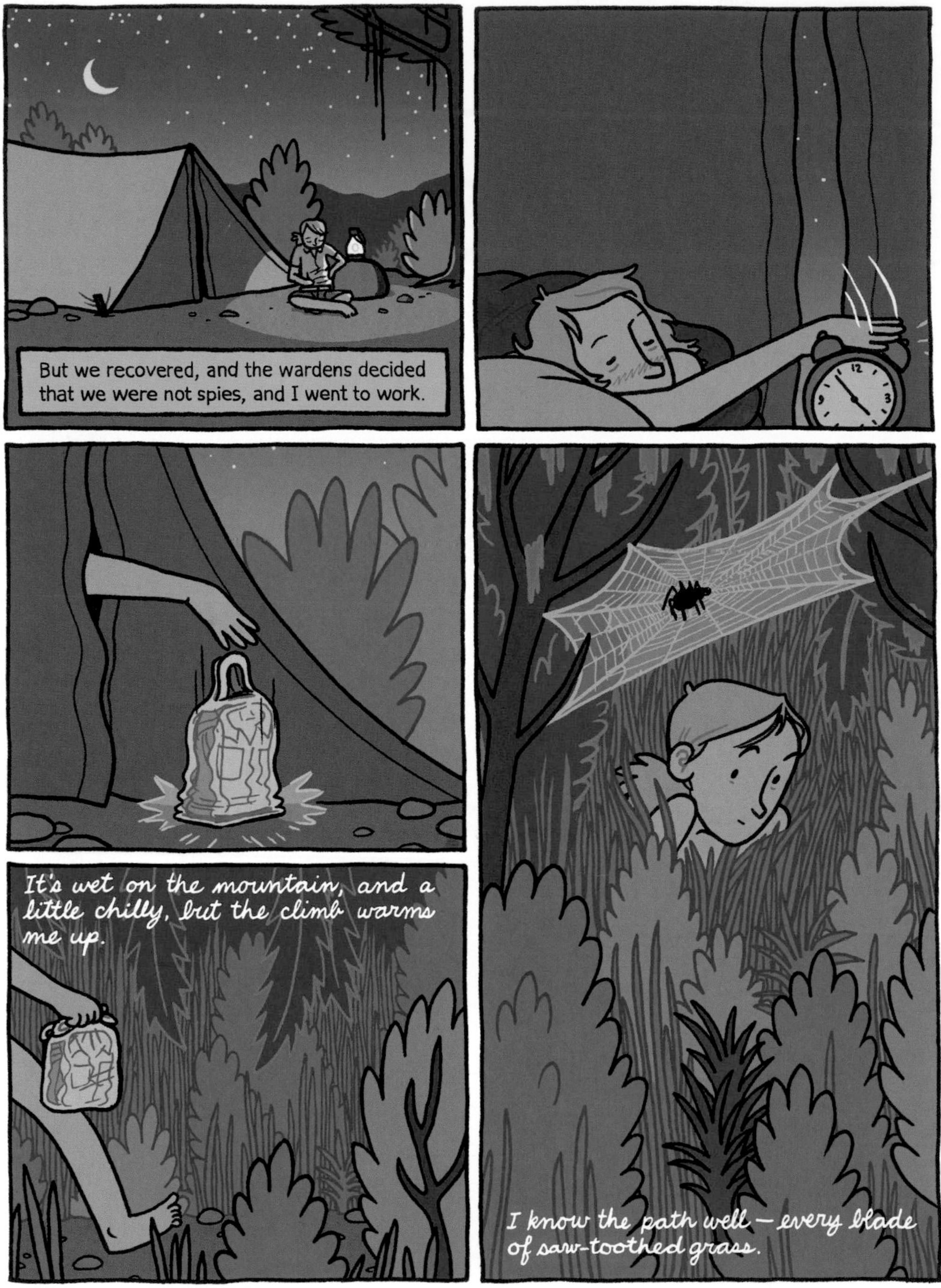
But we recovered, and the wardens decided that we were not spies, and I went to work.
12
3
9
It's wet on the mountain, and a little chilly, but the climb warms me up.
I know the path well — every blade of saw-toothed grass.

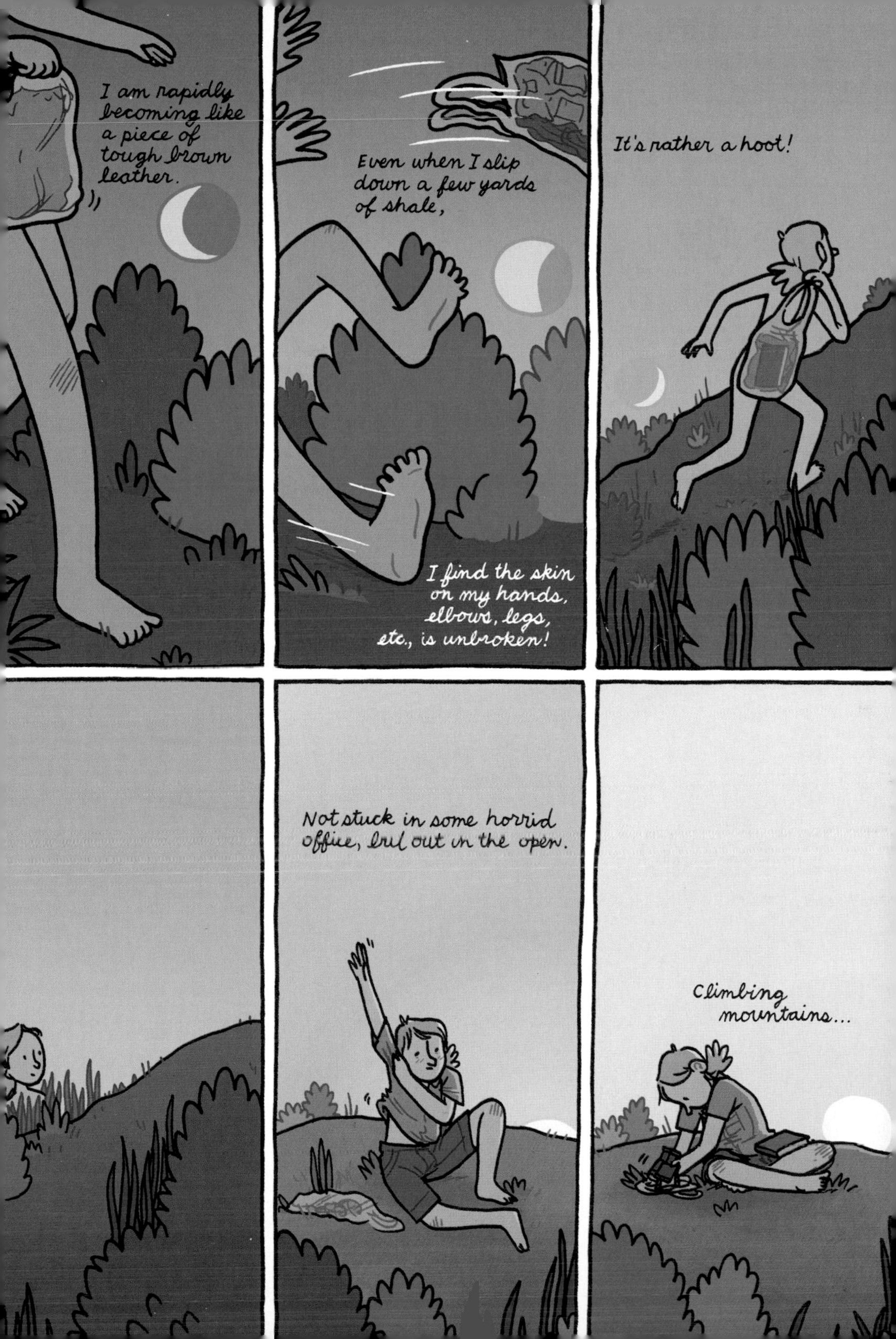
I am rapidly becoming like a piece of tough brown leather.
Even when I slip down a few yards of shale,
I find the skin on my hands, elbows, legs, etc., is unbroken!
It's rather a hoot!
Not stuck in some horrid office, but out in the open.
Climbing mountains...

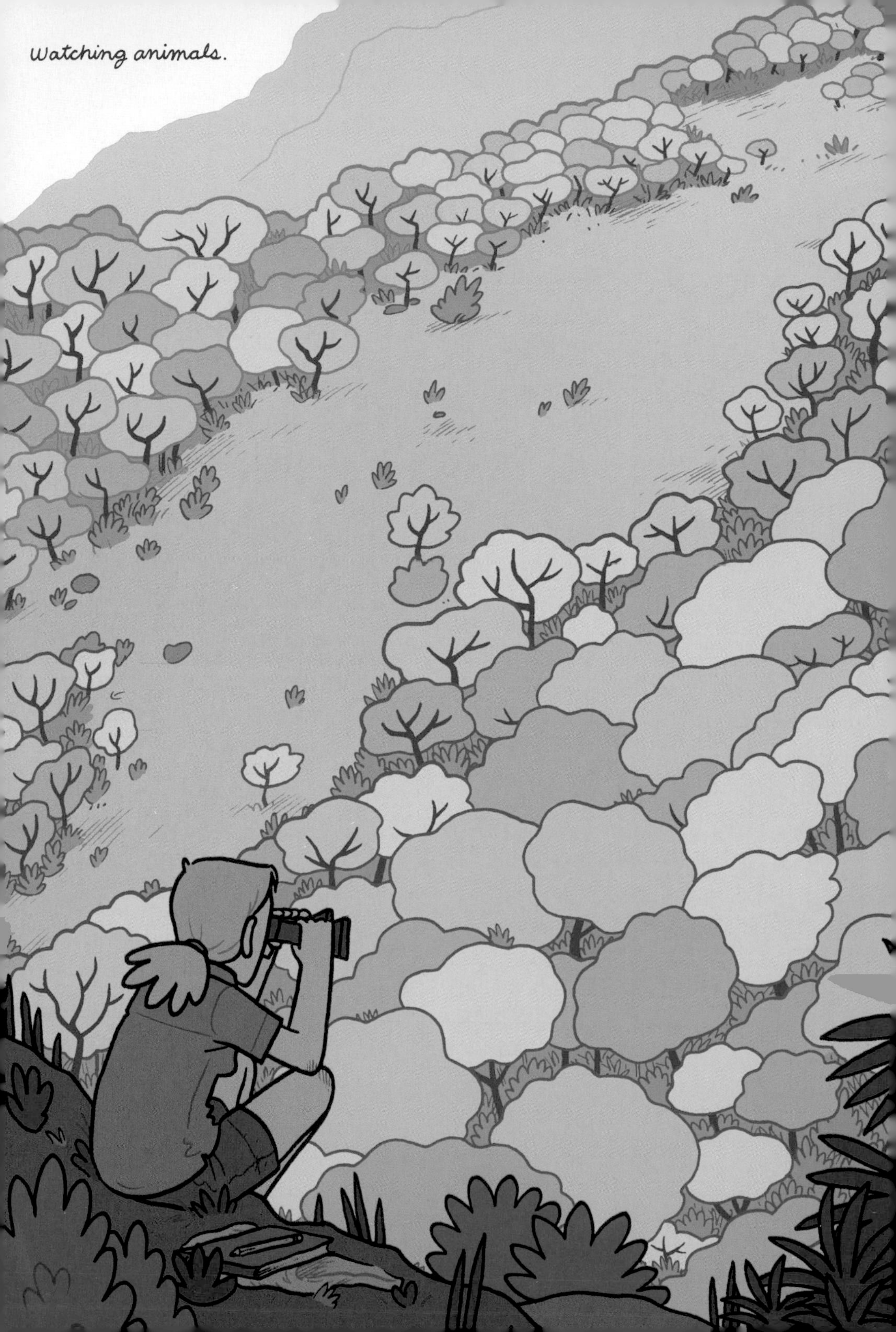
Watching animals.

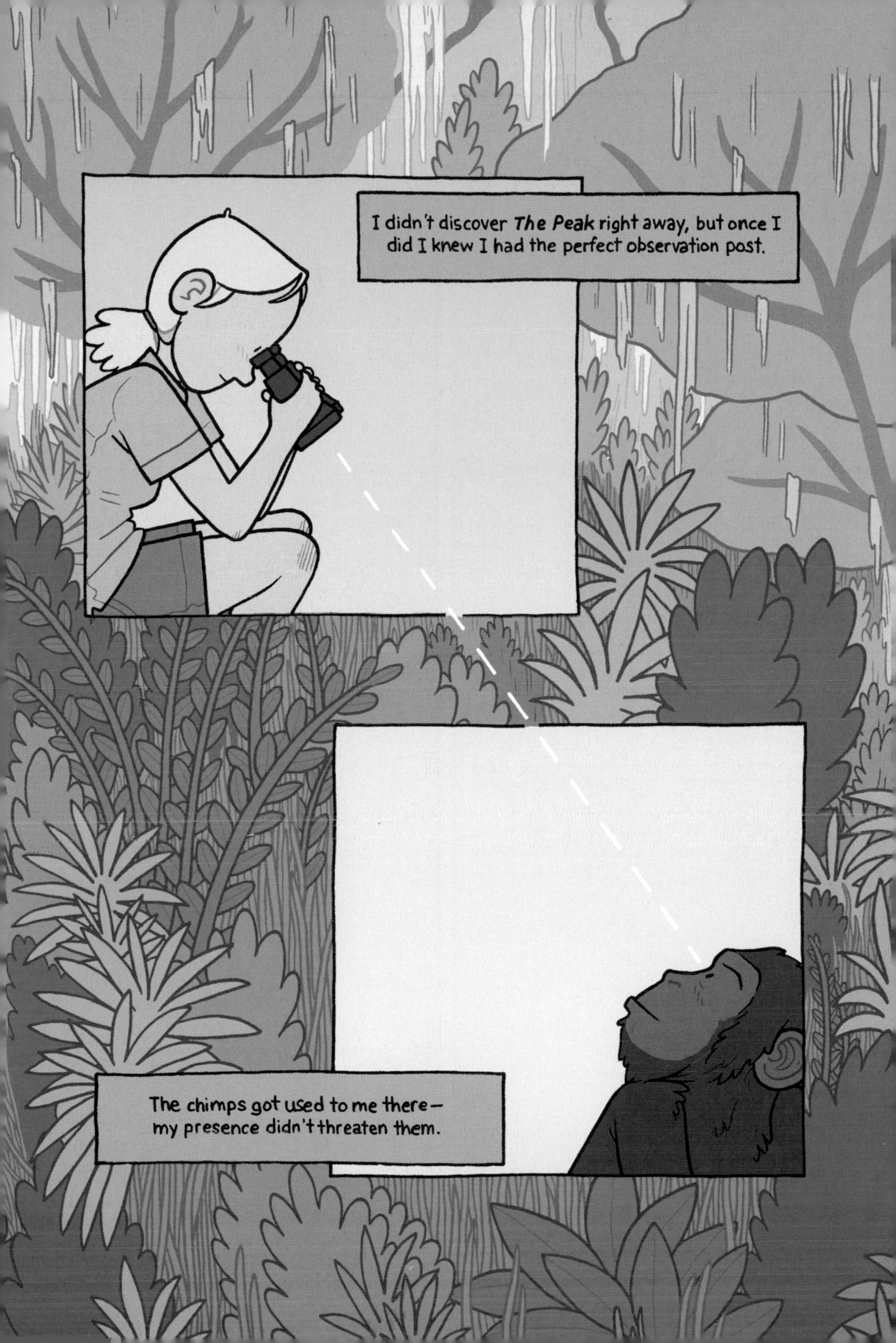
I didn't discover *The Peak* right away, but once I did I knew I had the perfect observation post.
The chimps got used to me there—my presence didn't threaten them.

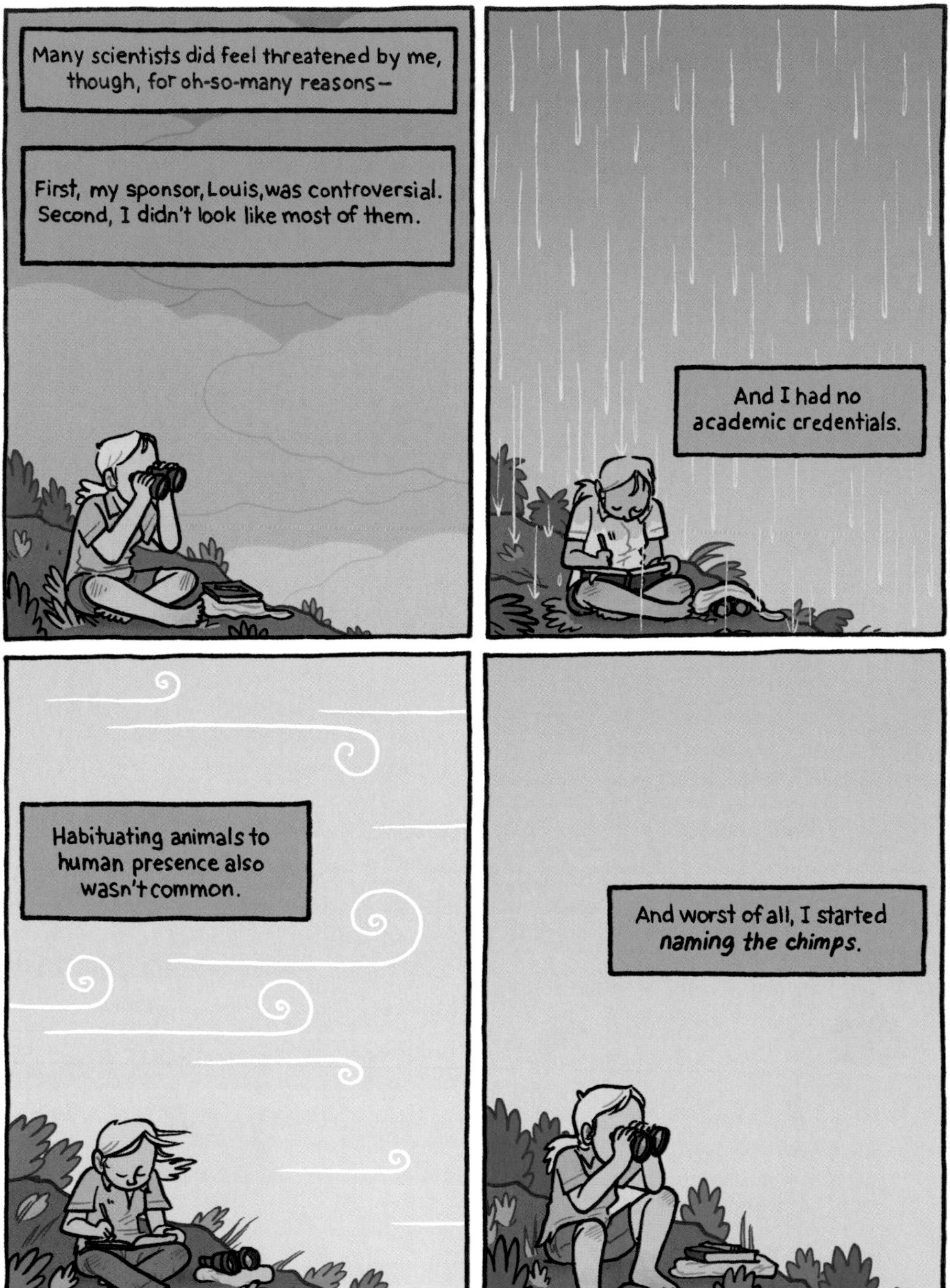
Many scientists did feel threatened by me, though, for oh-so-many reasons–
First, my sponsor, Louis, was controversial. Second, I didn't look like most of them.
And I had no academic credentials.
Habituating animals to human presence also wasn't common.
And worst of all, I started *naming the chimps*.

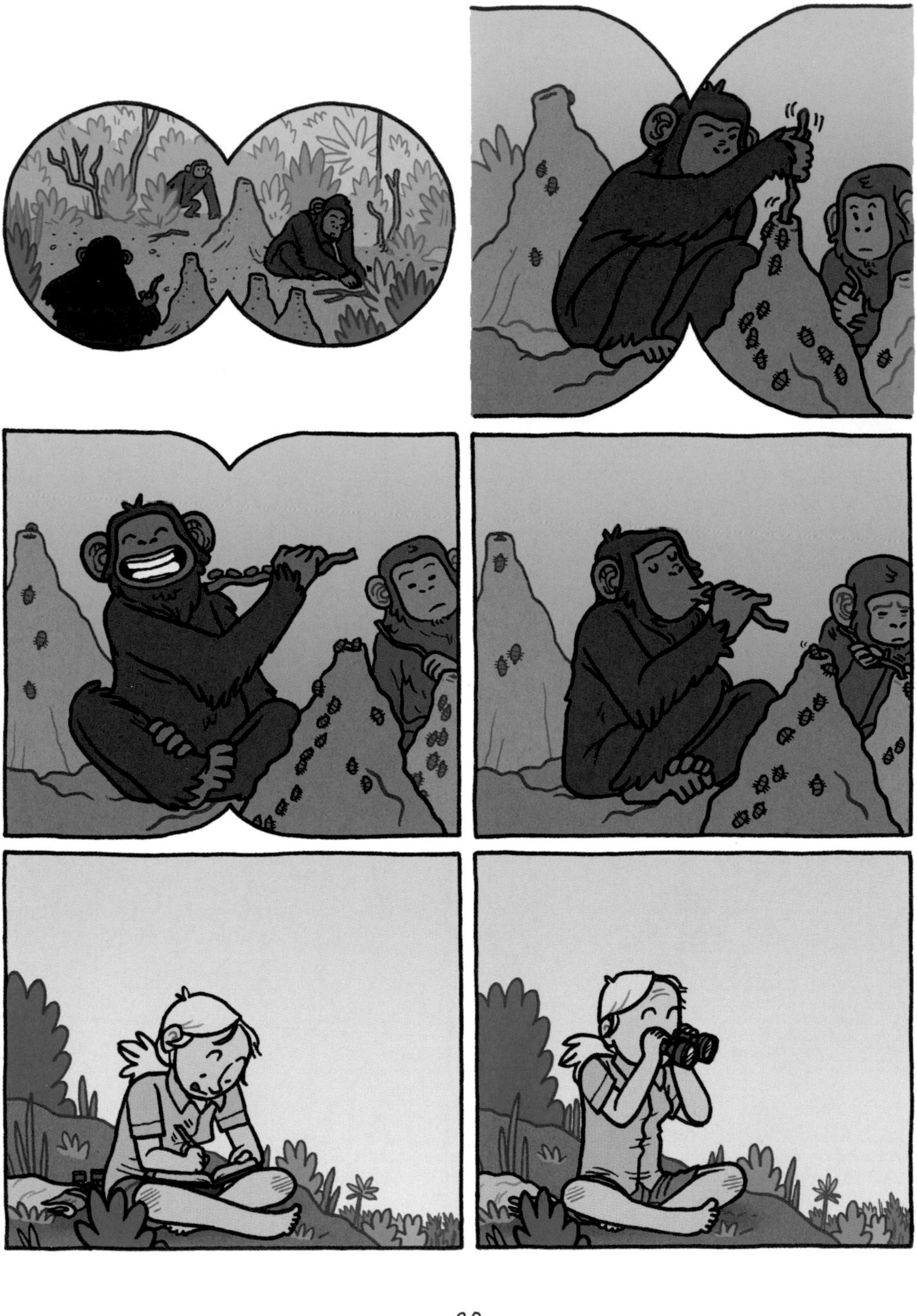

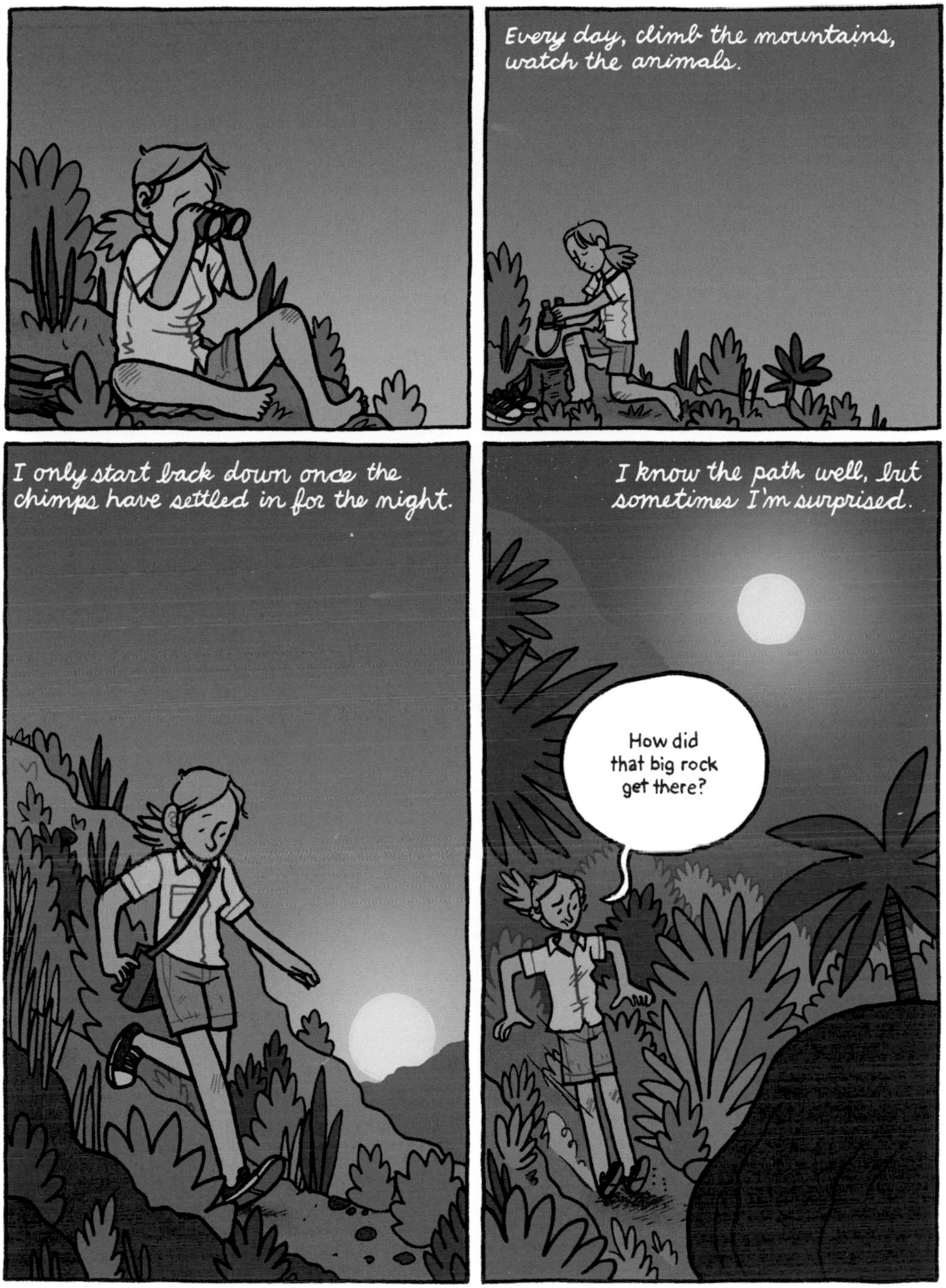

Every day, climb the mountains, watch the animals.
I only start back down once the chimps have settled in for the night.
I know the path well, but sometimes I'm surprised.
How did that big rock get there?

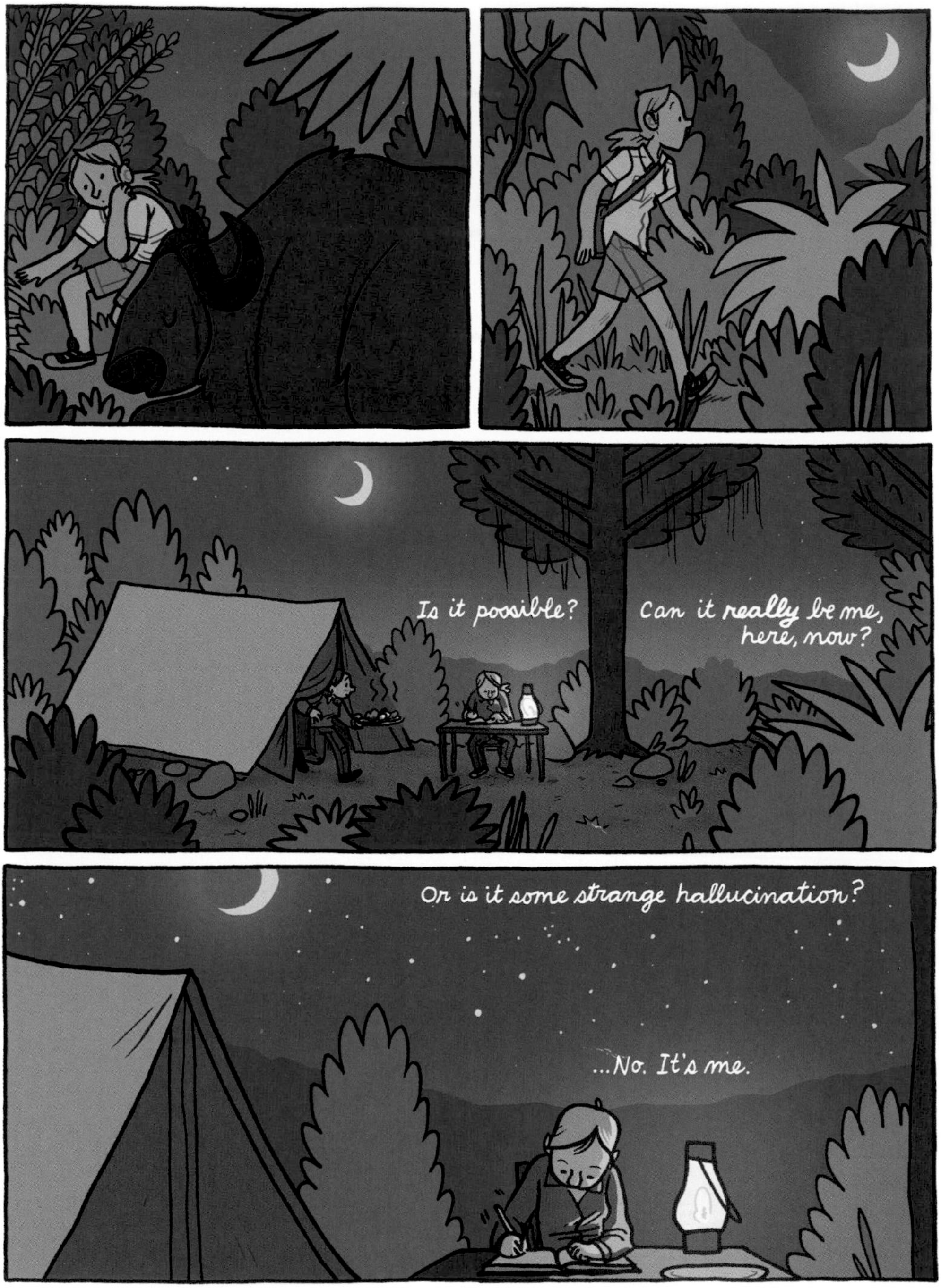
Is it possible?
Can it really be me, here, now?
Or is it some strange hallucination?
...No. It's me.

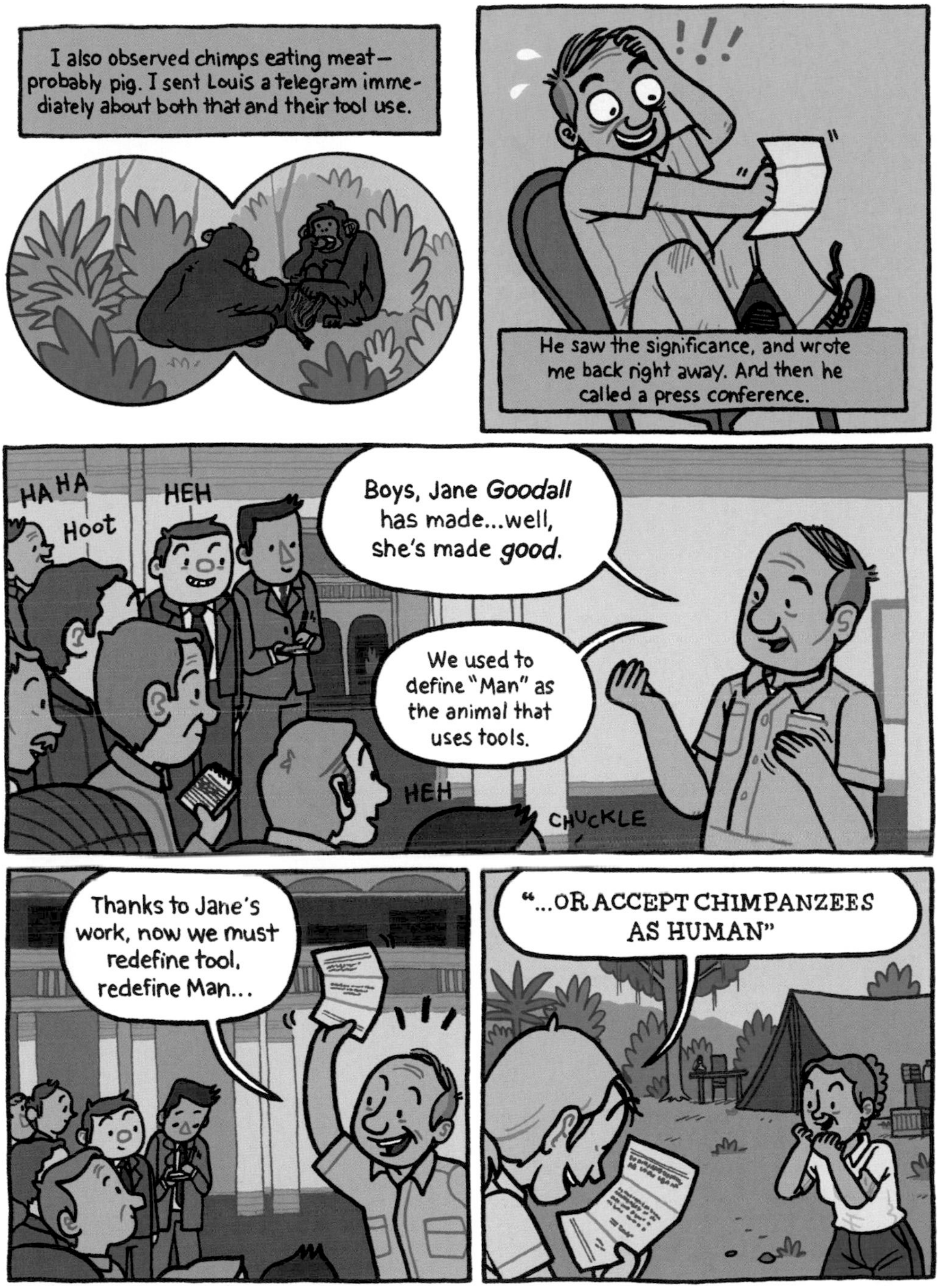
I also observed chimps eating meat—probably pig. I sent Louis a telegram immediately about both that and their tool use.
!!!
He saw the significance, and wrote me back right away. And then he called a press conference.
HA HA
Hoot
HEH
Boys, Jane Goodall has made...well, she's made good.
We used to define "Man" as the animal that uses tools.
HEH
CHUCKLE
Thanks to Jane's work, now we must redefine tool, redefine Man...
"...OR ACCEPT CHIMPANZEES AS HUMAN"

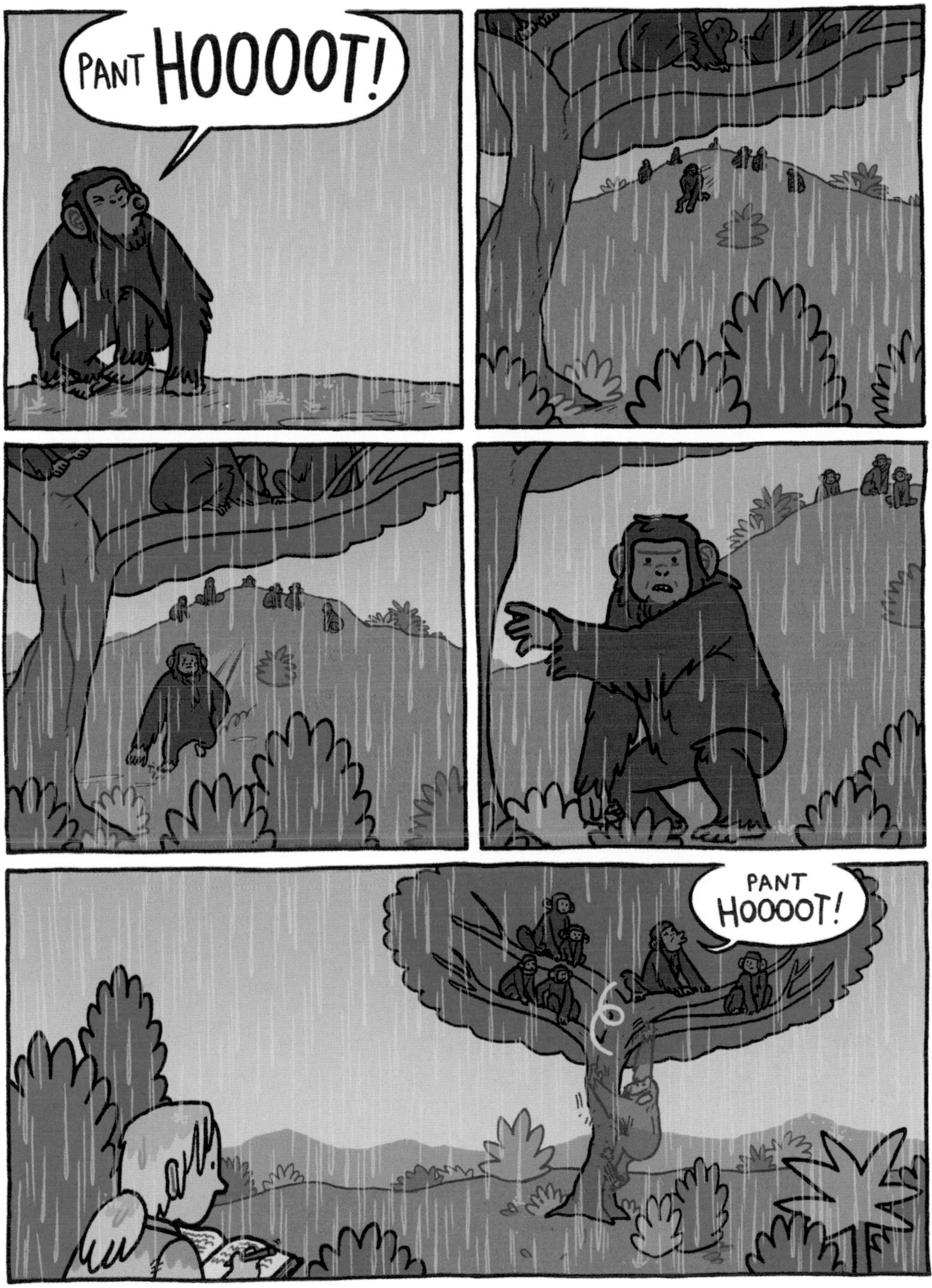
PANT HOOOOT!
PANT HOOOOT!

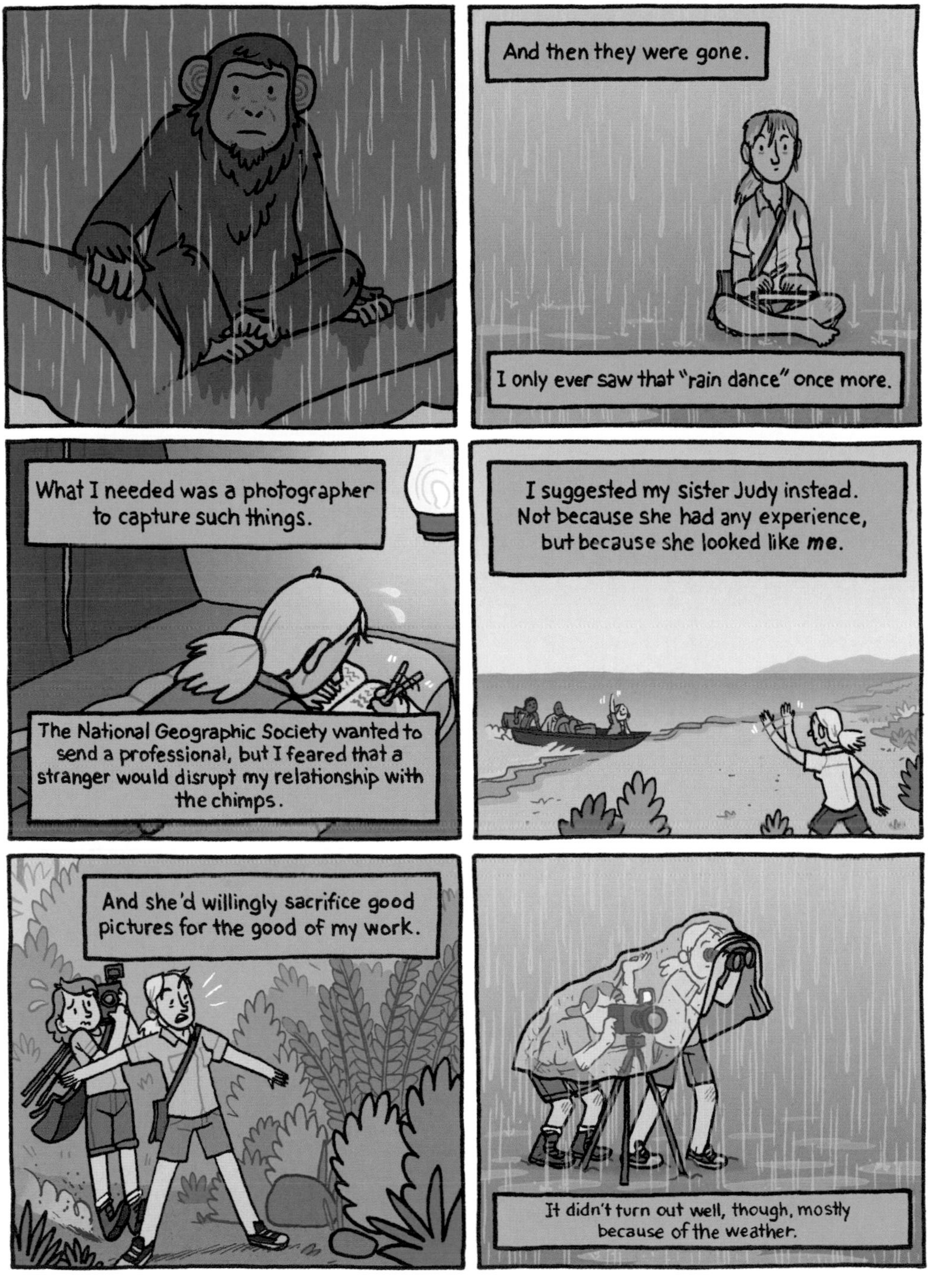
And then they were gone.
I only ever saw that "rain dance" once more.
What I needed was a photographer to capture such things.
The National Geographic Society wanted to send a professional, but I feared that a stranger would disrupt my relationship with the chimps.
I suggested my sister Judy instead. Not because she had any experience, but because she looked like *me*.
And she'd willingly sacrifice good pictures for the good of my work.
It didn't turn out well, though, mostly because of the weather.

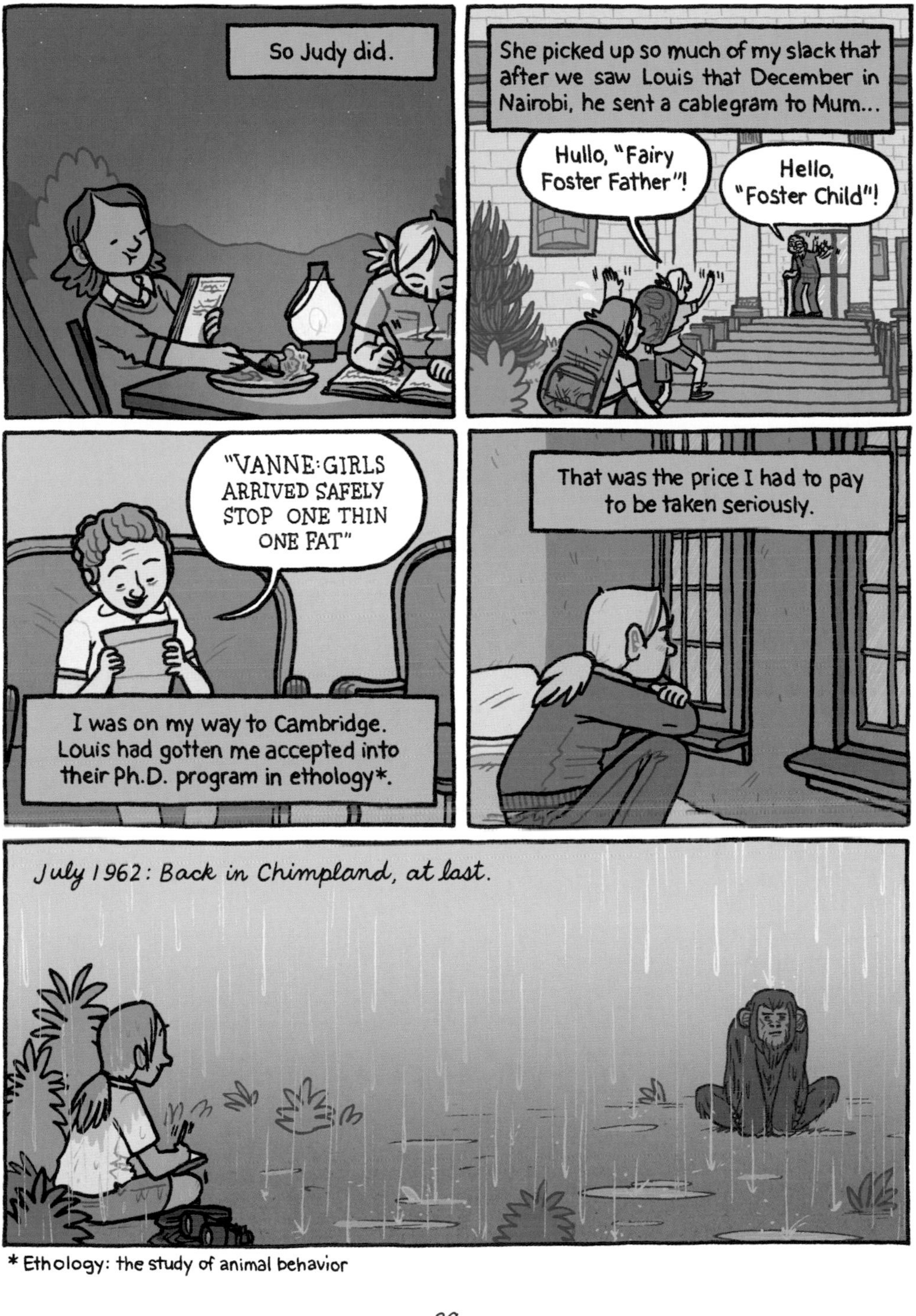
So Judy did.
She picked up so much of my slack that after we saw Louis that December in Nairobi, he sent a cablegram to Mum...
Hullo, "Fairy Foster Father"!
Hello, "Foster Child"!
"VANNE: GIRLS ARRIVED SAFELY STOP ONE THIN ONE FAT"
I was on my way to Cambridge. Louis had gotten me accepted into their Ph.D. program in ethology*.
That was the price I had to pay to be taken seriously.
July 1962: Back in Chimpland, at last.

* Ethology: the study of animal behavior

* Working with dung, again!

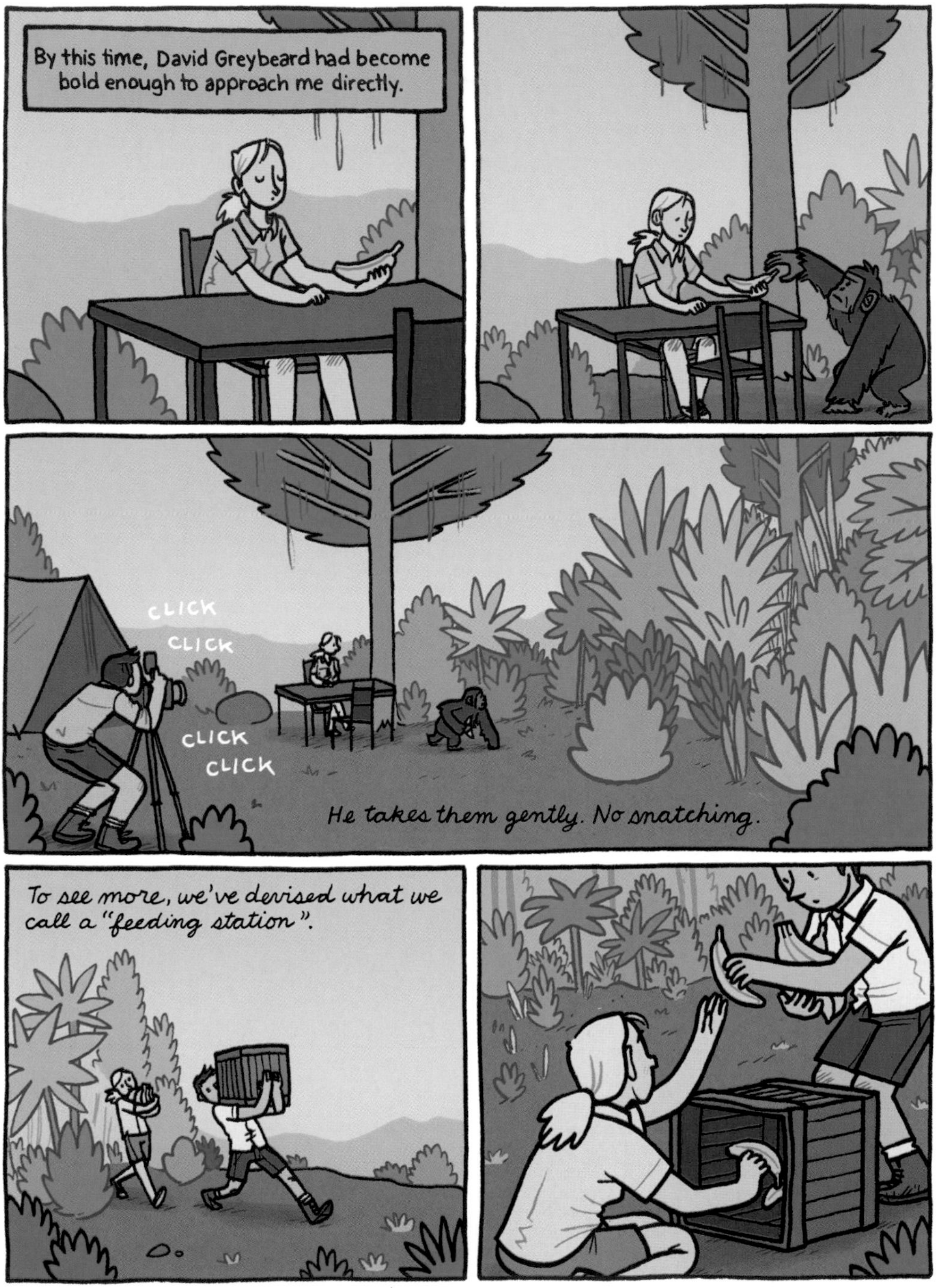
By this time, David Greybeard had become bold enough to approach me directly.
CLICK
CLICK
CLICK
CLICK
He takes them gently. No snatching.
To see more, we've devised what we call a "feeding station".

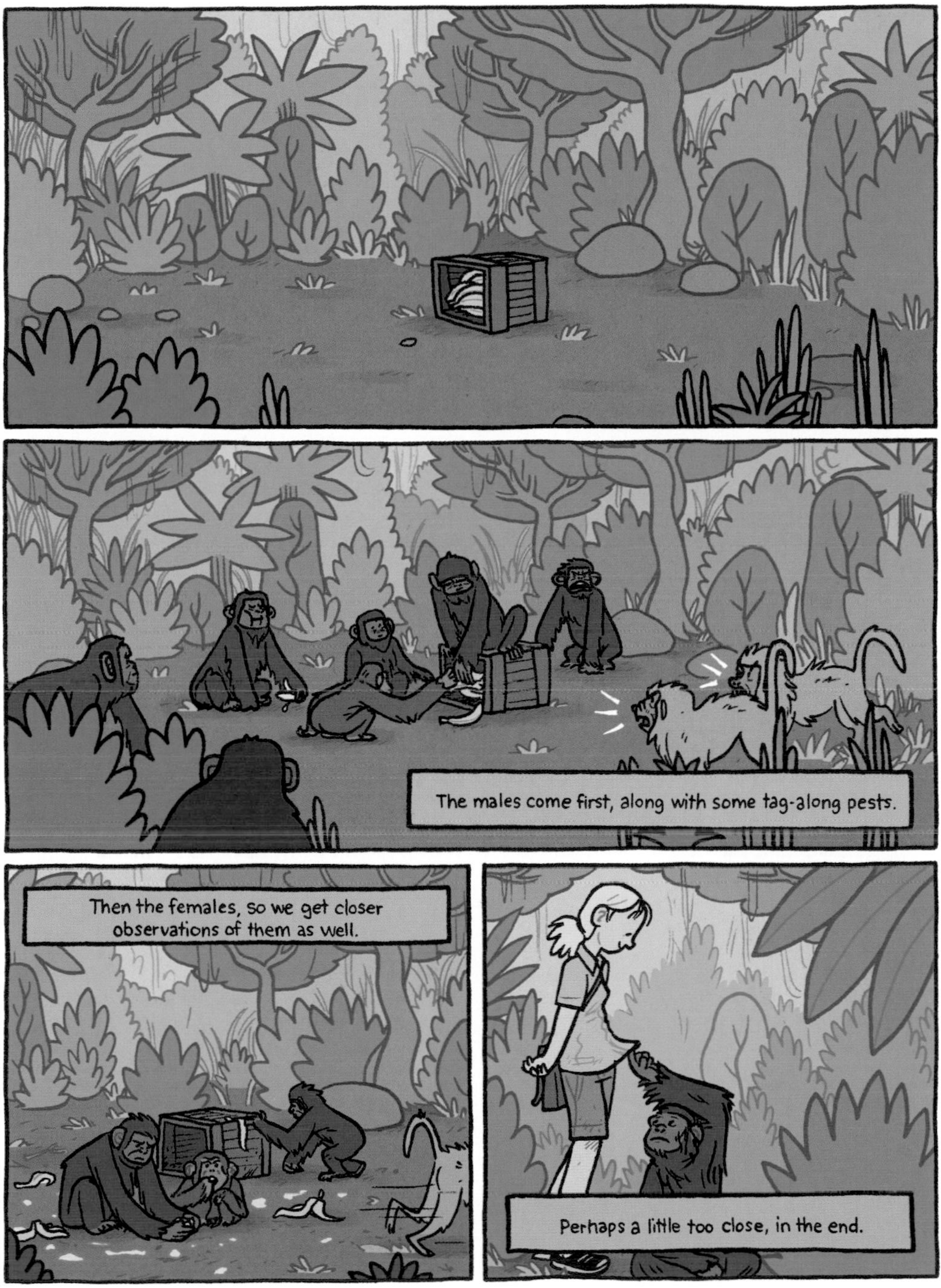
The males come first, along with some tag-along pests.
Then the females, so we get closer observations of them as well.
Perhaps a little too close, in the end.

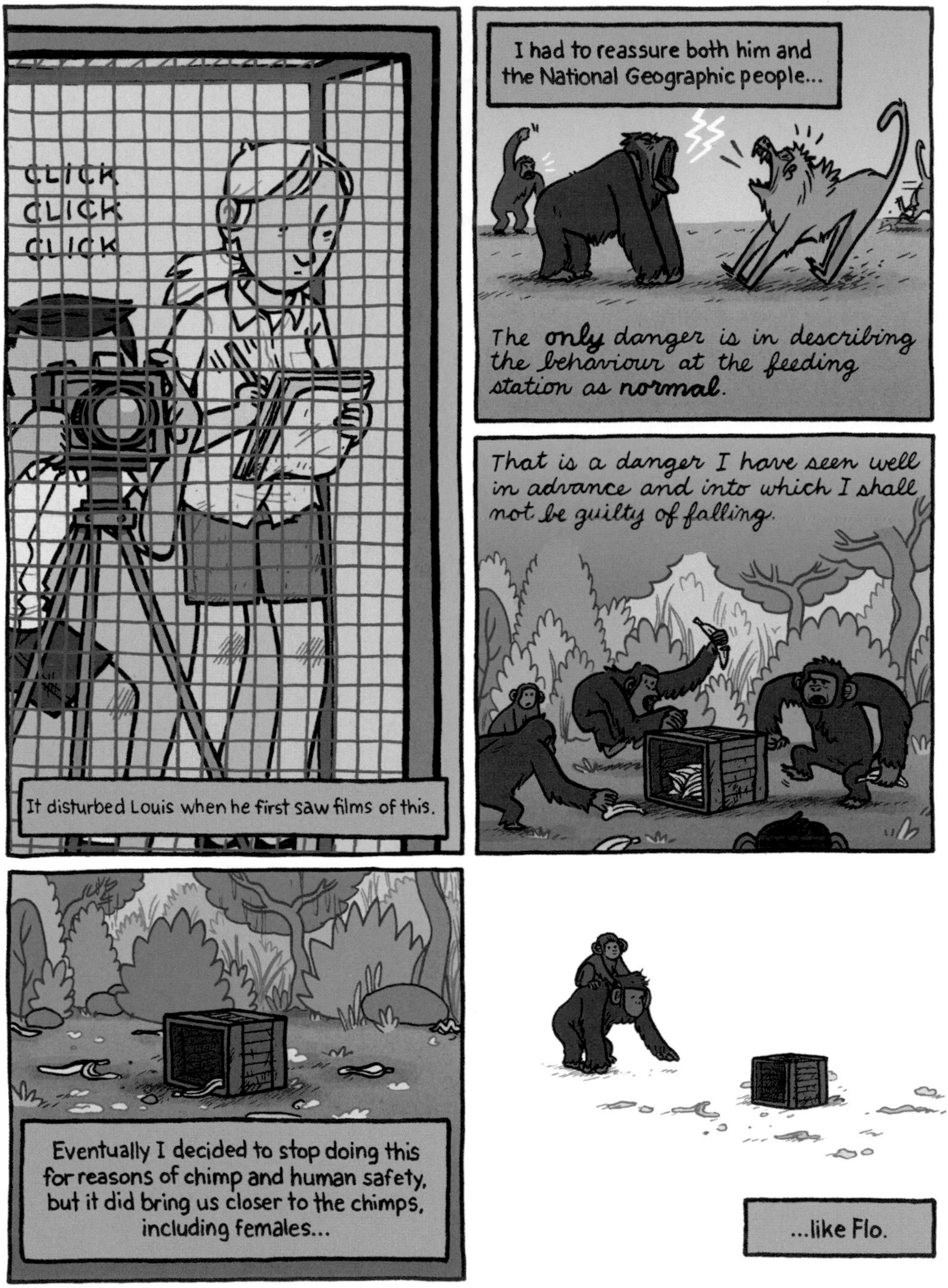
CLICK
CLICK
CLICK
It disturbed Louis when he first saw films of this.
I had to reassure both him and the National Geographic people...
The only danger is in describing the behaviour at the feeding station as normal.
That is a danger I have seen well in advance and into which I shall not be guilty of falling.
Eventually I decided to stop doing this for reasons of chimp and human safety, but it did bring us closer to the chimps, including females...
...like Flo.

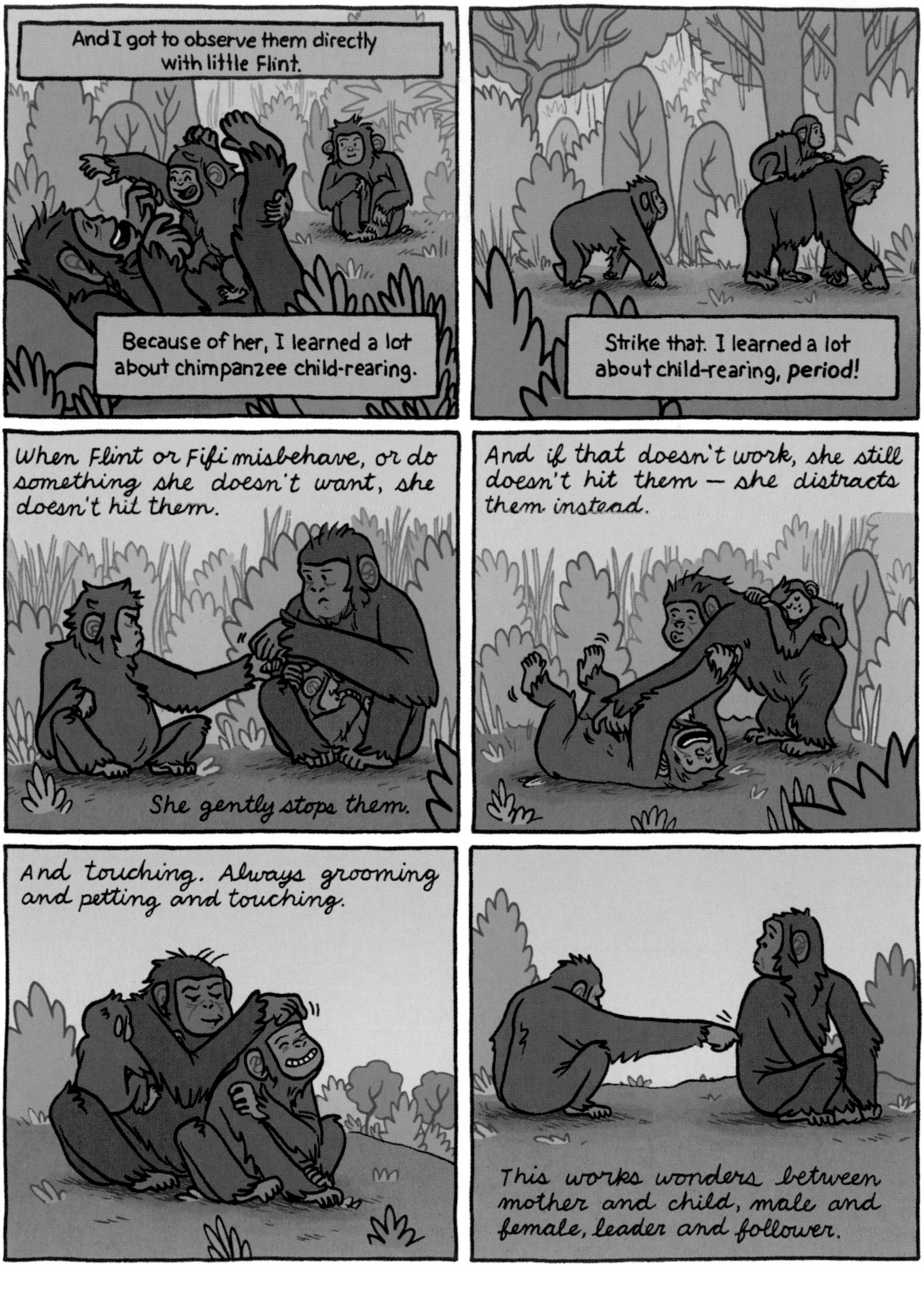

And I got to observe them directly with little Flint.
Because of her, I learned a lot about chimpanzee child-rearing.
Strike that. I learned a lot about child-rearing, period!
When Flint or Fifi misbehave, or do something she doesn't want, she doesn't hit them.
She gently stops them.
And if that doesn't work, she still doesn't hit them — she distracts them instead.
And touching. Always grooming and petting and touching.
This works wonders between mother and child, male and female, leader and follower.

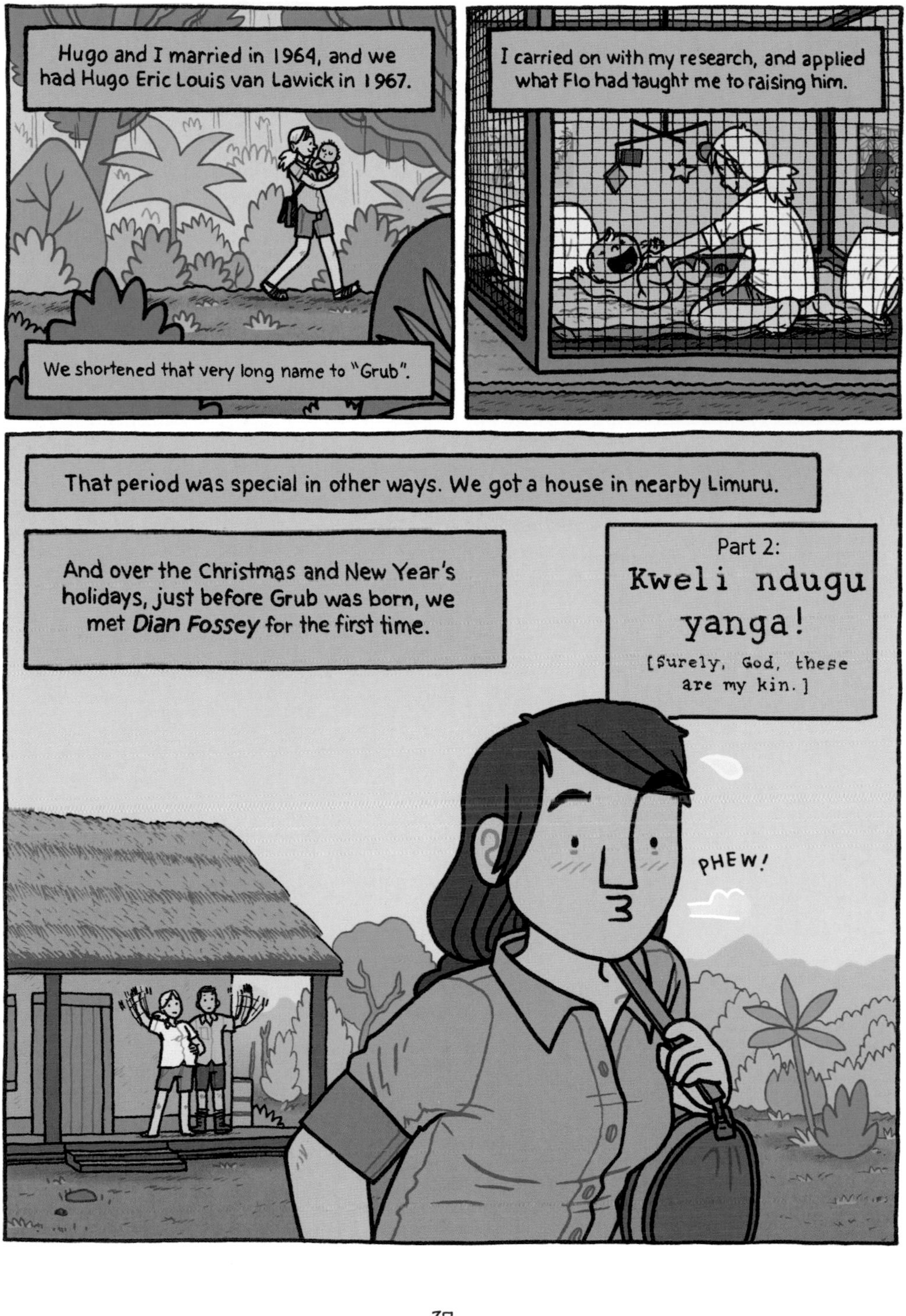
Hugo and I married in 1964, and we had Hugo Eric Louis van Lawick in 1967.
We shortened that very long name to "Grub".
I carried on with my research, and applied what Flo had taught me to raising him.
That period was special in other ways. We got a house in nearby Limuru.
And over the Christmas and New Year's holidays, just before Grub was born, we met *Dian Fossey* for the first time.
Part 2:
Kweli ndugu yanga!
[Surely, God, these are my kin.]
PHEW!

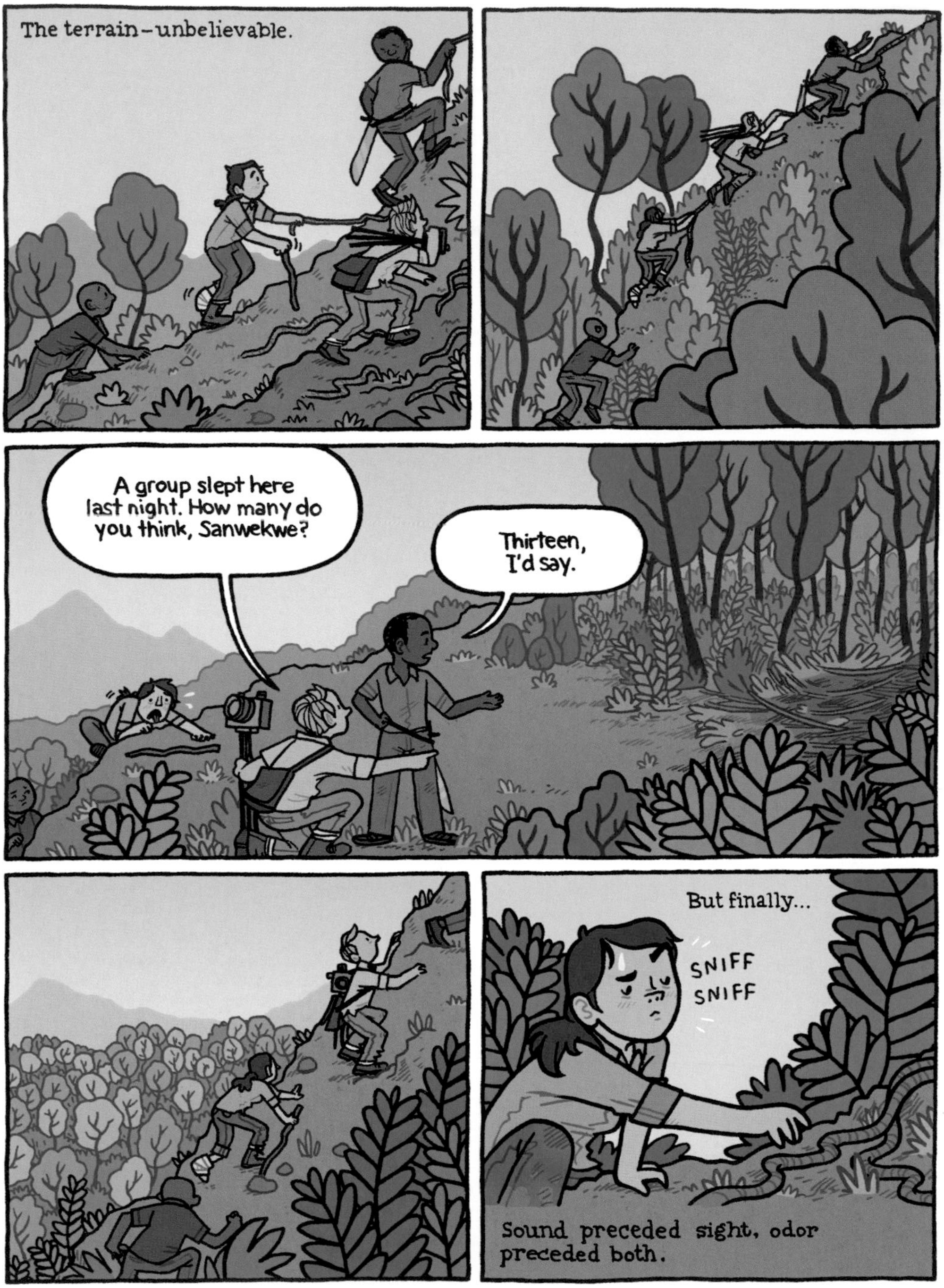
The terrain—unbelievable.
A group slept here last night. How many do you think, Sanwekwe?
Thirteen, I'd say.
But finally...
SNIFF SNIFF
Sound preceded sight, odor preceded both.

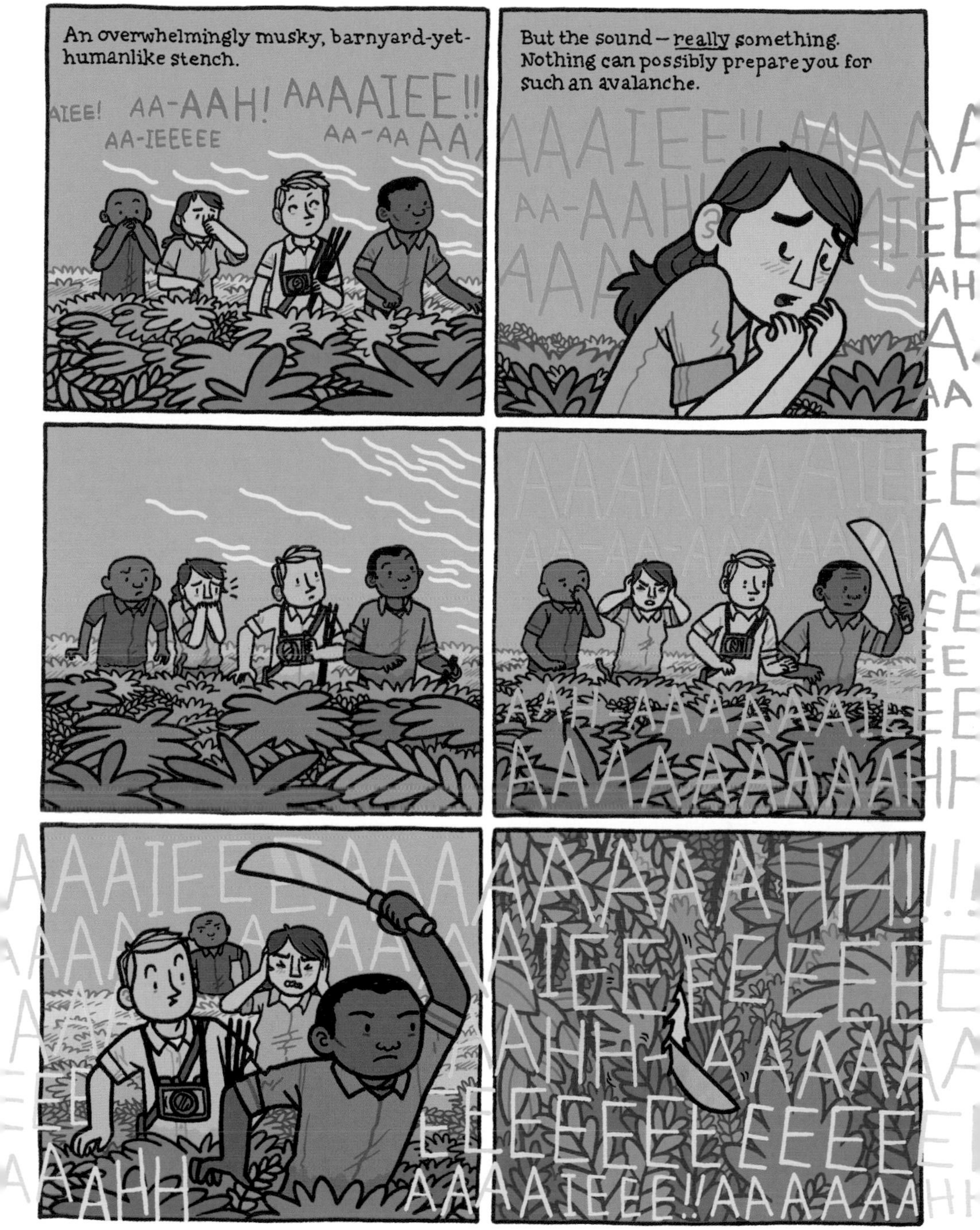
An overwhelmingly musky, barnyard-yet-humanlike stench.
AIEE! AA-AAH! AAAAIEE!!
AA-IEEEEE
AA-AA AA
But the sound — really something. Nothing can possibly prepare you for such an avalanche.
AAAIEE!!
AA-AAH!
AAAAAAHH!!
AIEEEEEEEEE
AAHH-AAAAA
AAAAIEEEE!! AAAAAAA
AAHH

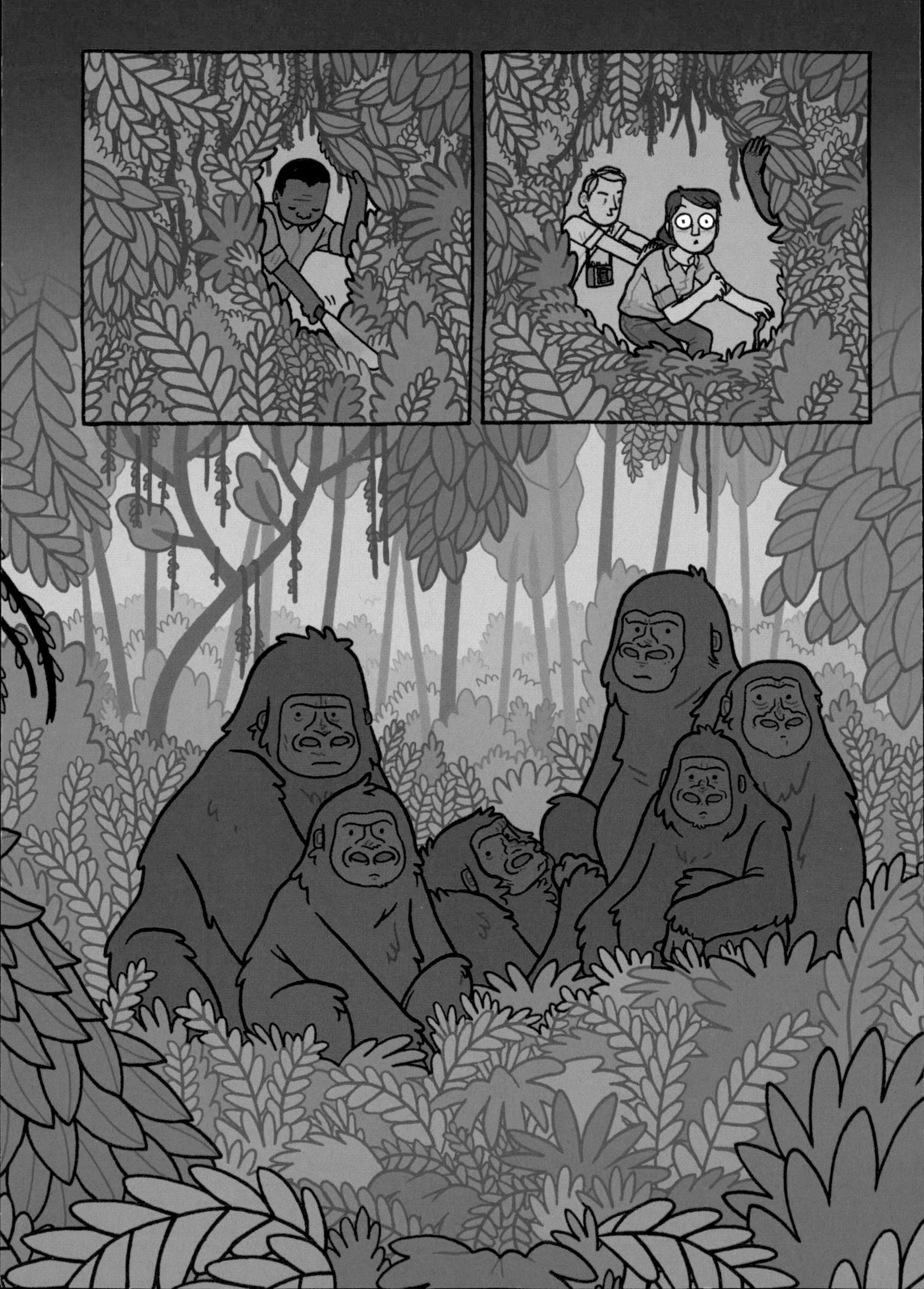

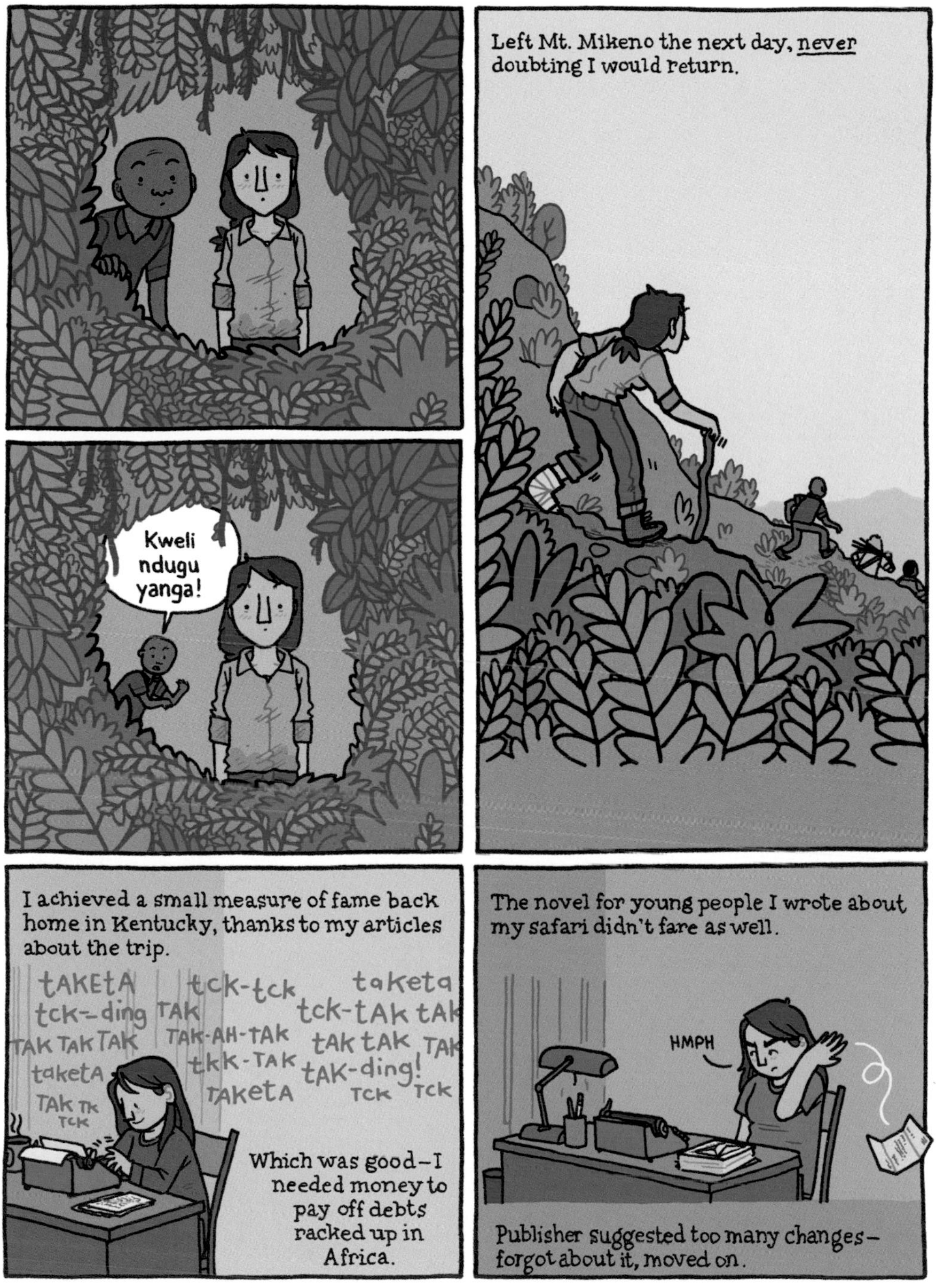
Left Mt. Mikeno the next day, never doubting I would return.
Kweli ndugu yanga!
I achieved a small measure of fame back home in Kentucky, thanks to my articles about the trip.
tAKEtA tck-tck taketa tck-ding TAK tck-tAk tAk TAK TAK TAK TAK-AH-TAK tAk tAk TAK taketA tkk-TAK tAK-ding! TAK TK TCK TAKETA TCK TCK
Which was good—I needed money to pay off debts racked up in Africa.
The novel for young people I wrote about my safari didn't fare as well.
HMPH
Publisher suggested too many changes—forgot about it, moved on.

45

46

48

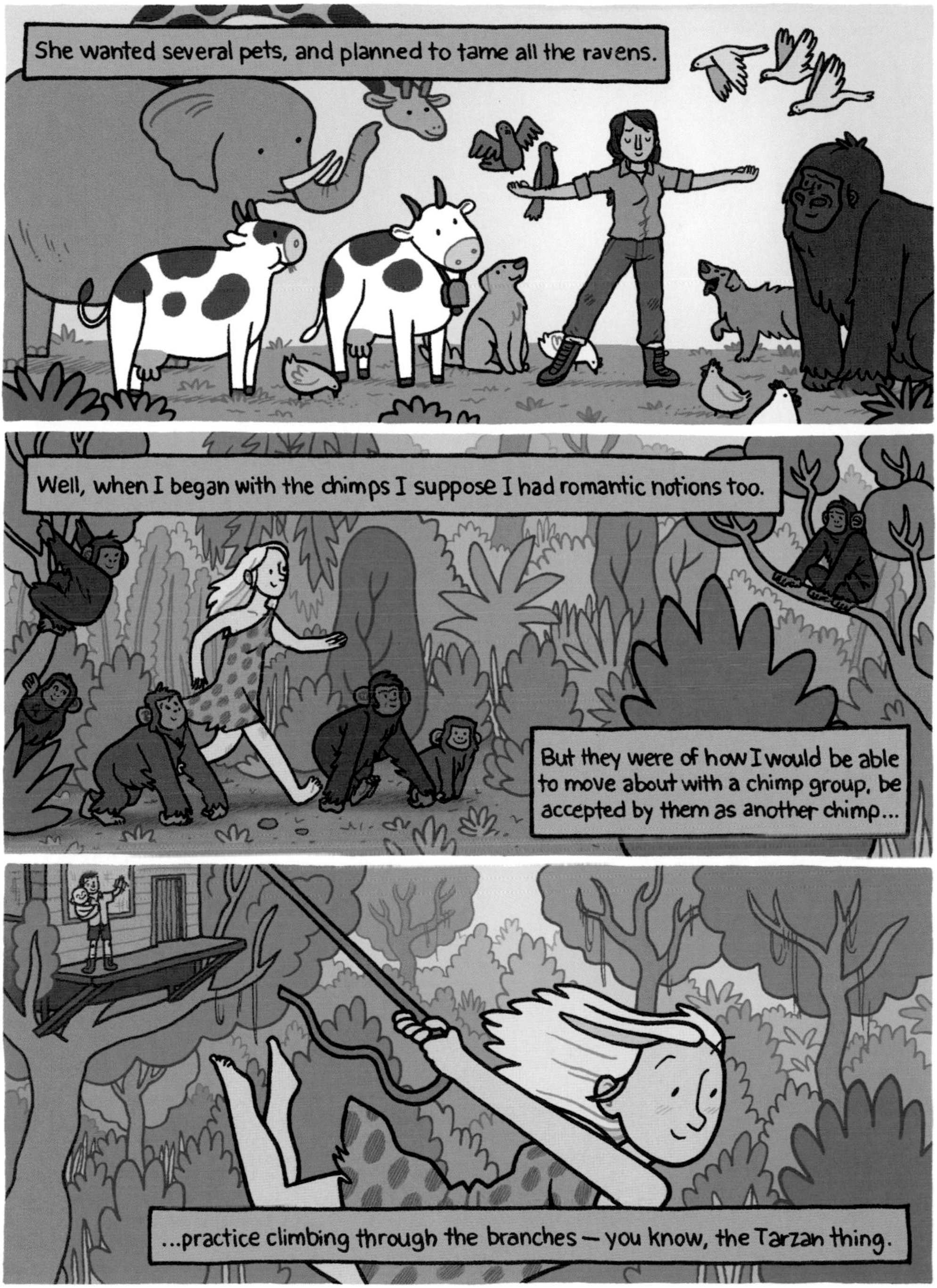
She wanted several pets, and planned to tame all the ravens.
Well, when I began with the chimps I suppose I had romantic notions too.
But they were of how I would be able to move about with a chimp group, be accepted by them as another chimp...
...practice climbing through the branches – you know, the Tarzan thing.

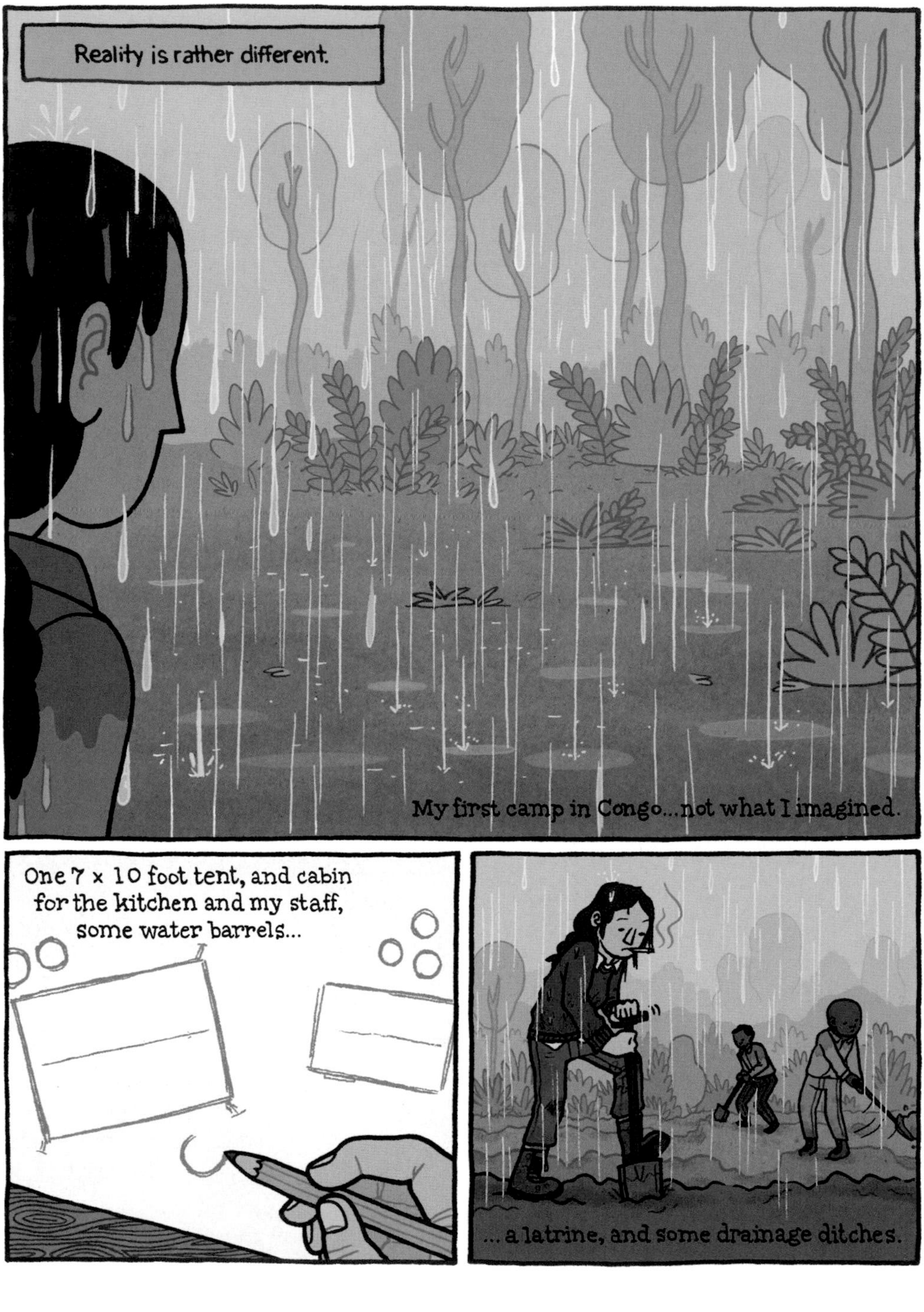
Reality is rather different.
My first camp in Congo... not what I imagined.
One 7 x 10 foot tent, and cabin for the kitchen and my staff, some water barrels...
... a latrine, and some drainage ditches.

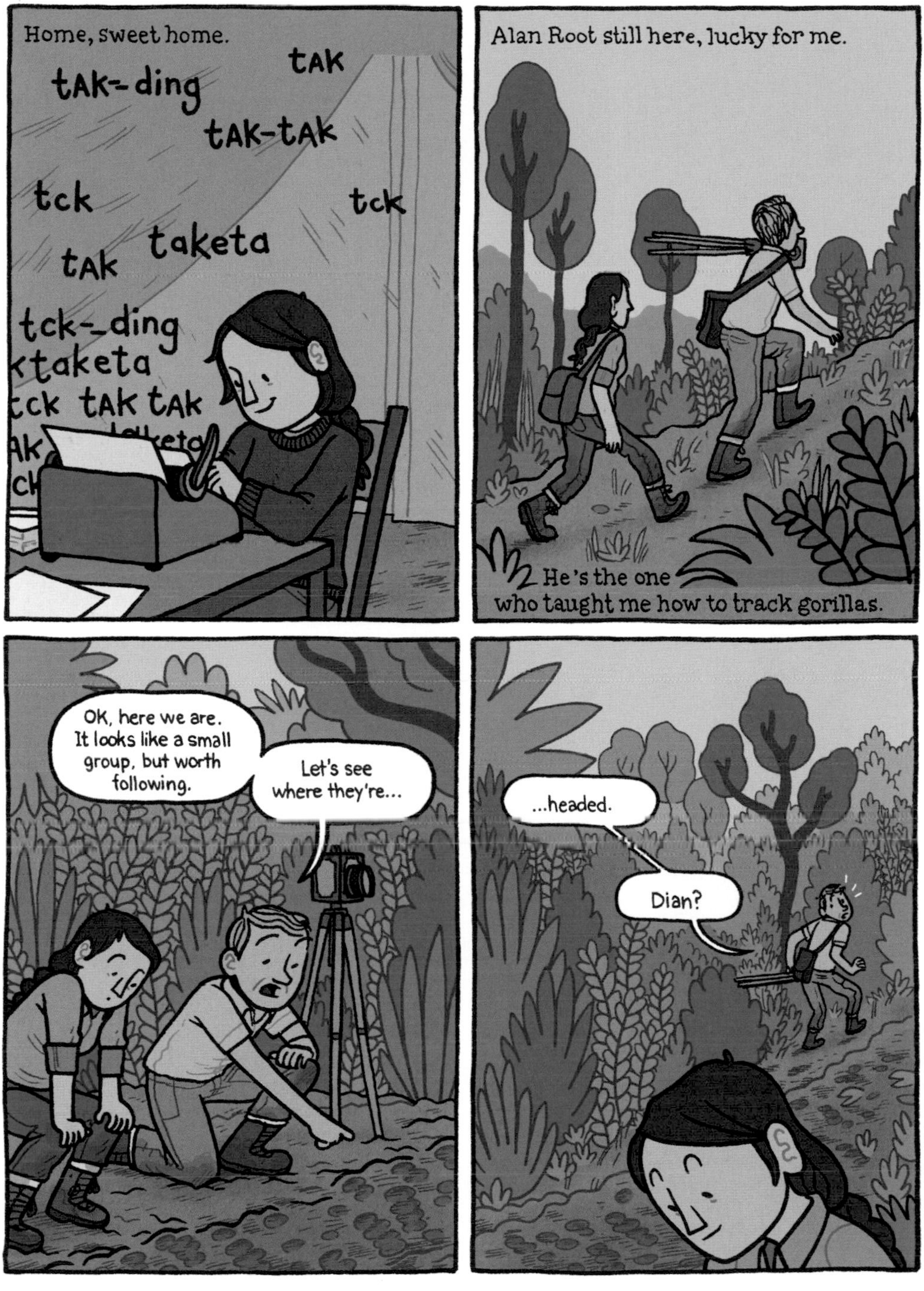
Home, sweet home.
tAK-ding
tAK
tAK-tAK
tck
tck
tAK
taketa
tck-ding
taketa
tAK tAK
Alan Root still here, lucky for me.
He's the one who taught me how to track gorillas.
OK, here we are. It looks like a small group, but worth following.
Let's see where they're...
...headed.
Dian?

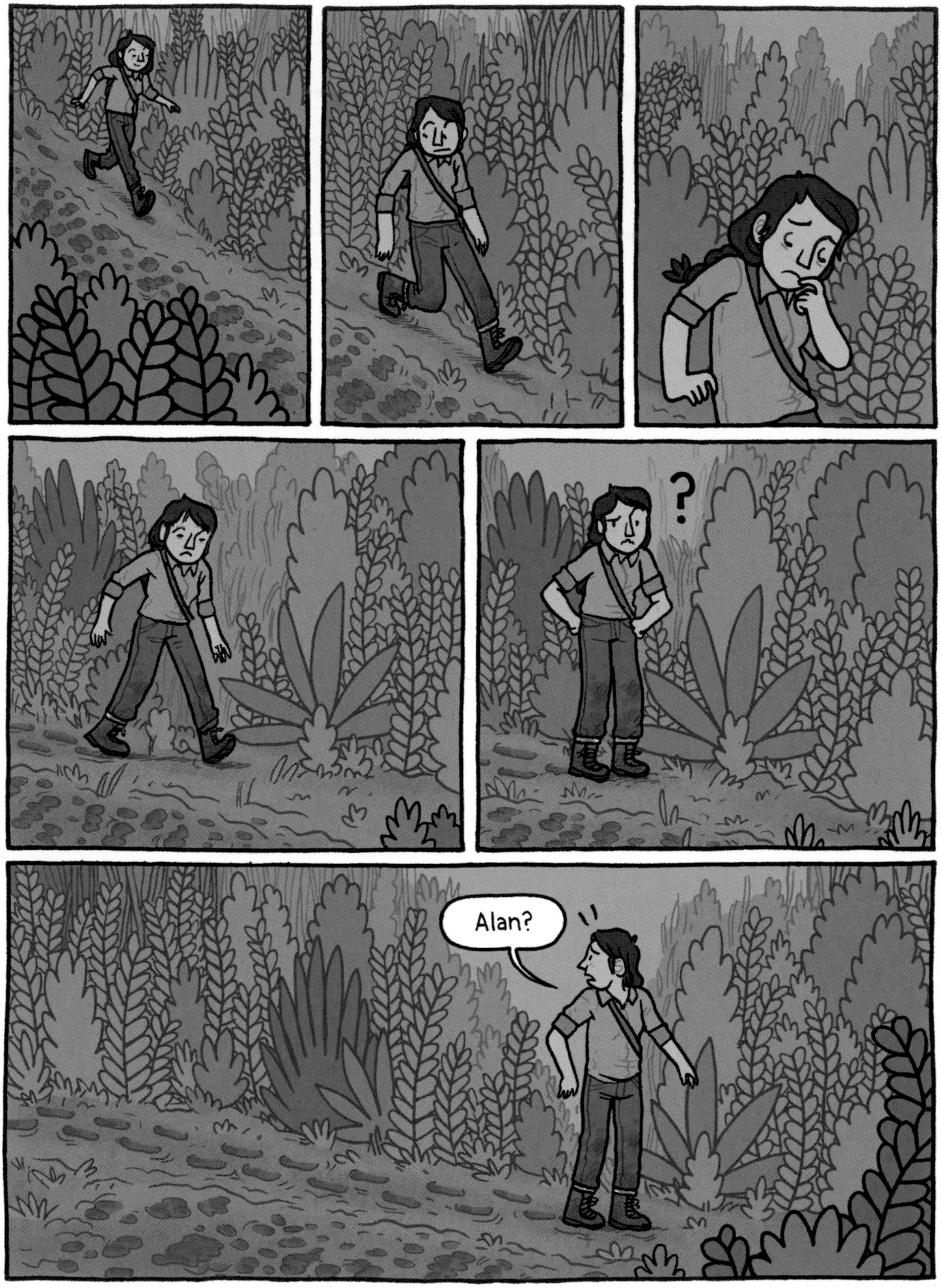
?
Alan?

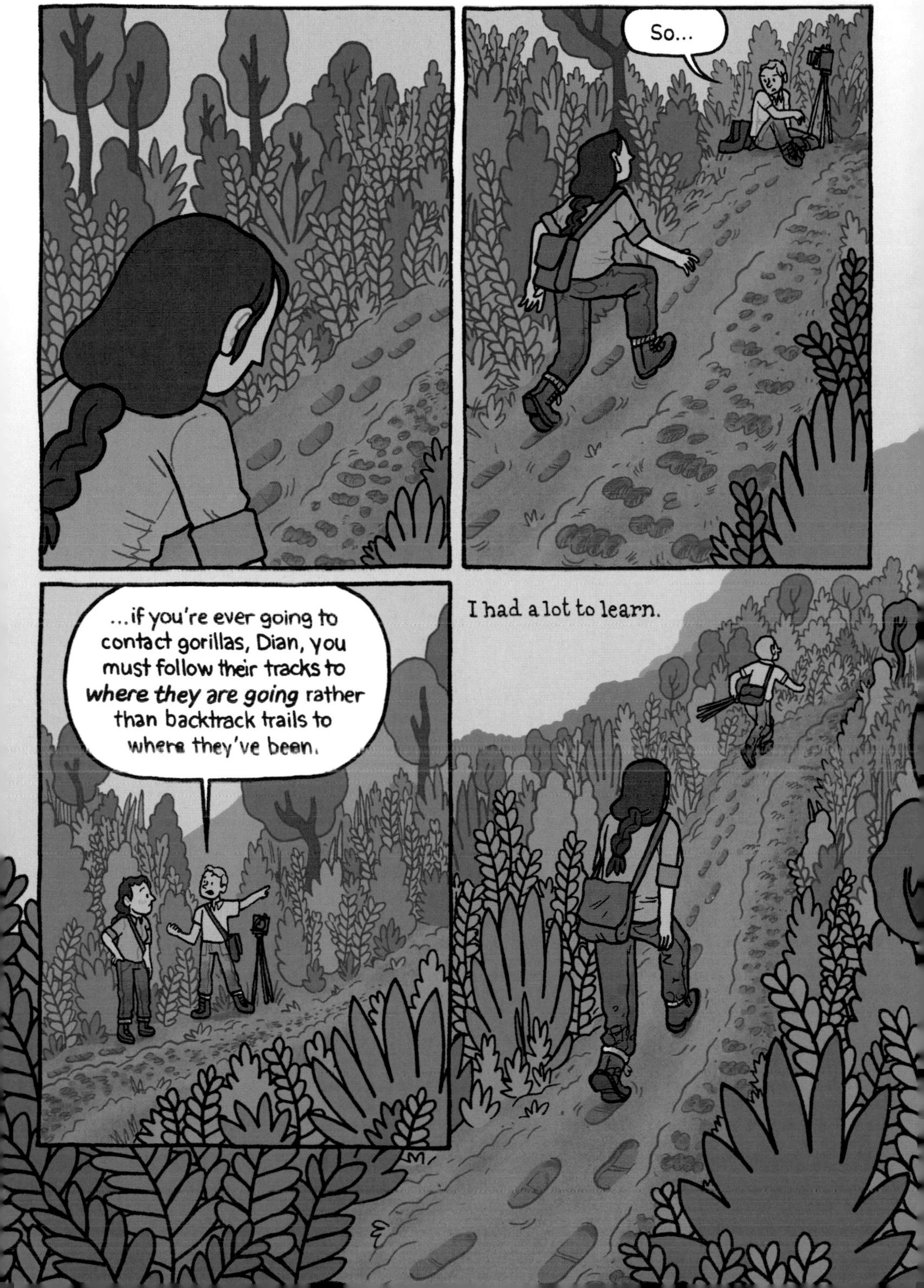
So...
...if you're ever going to contact gorillas, Dian, you must follow their tracks to *where they are going* rather than backtrack trails to where they've been.
I had a lot to learn.

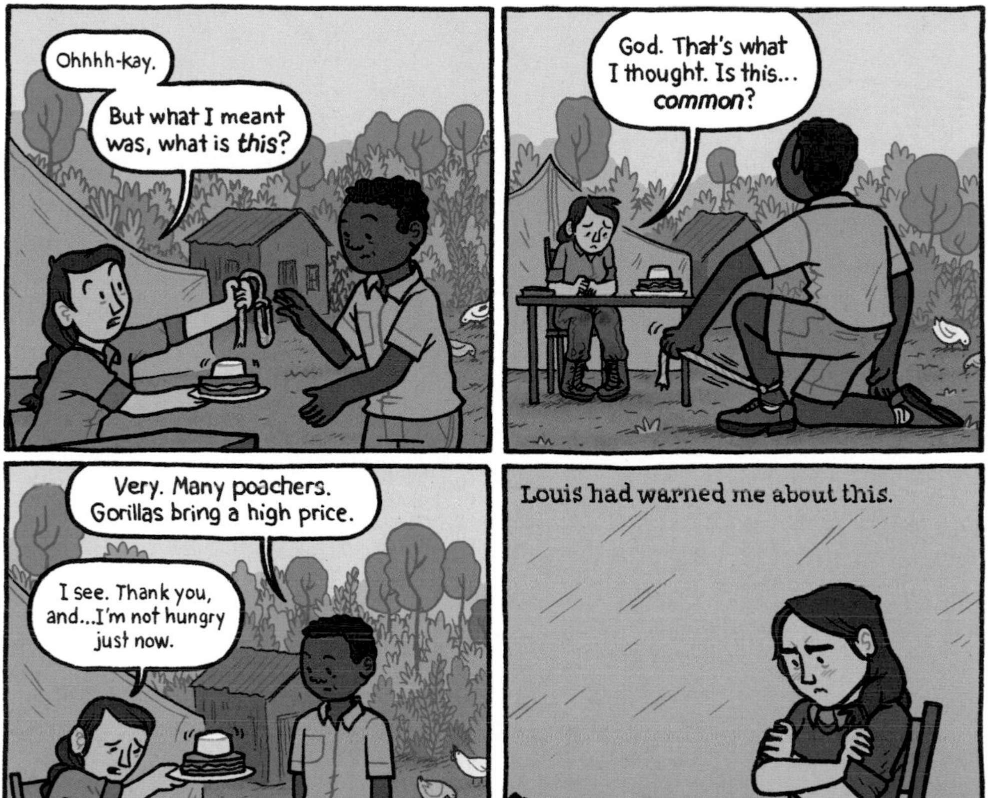

Ohhhh-kay.
But what I meant was, what is *this*?
God. That's what I thought. Is this... *common*?
Very. Many poachers. Gorillas bring a high price.
I see. Thank you, and...I'm not hungry just now.
Louis had warned me about this.
It just won't do.
TAK
TAK-- ding
TAK TCK
TAKETA
TAKETA
TAK T
ding
TCK TAK TAK
TCK
July 7, 1967: Other problems to deal with first, though. Been told to leave Congo by the park director.
White people no longer welcome in the country.

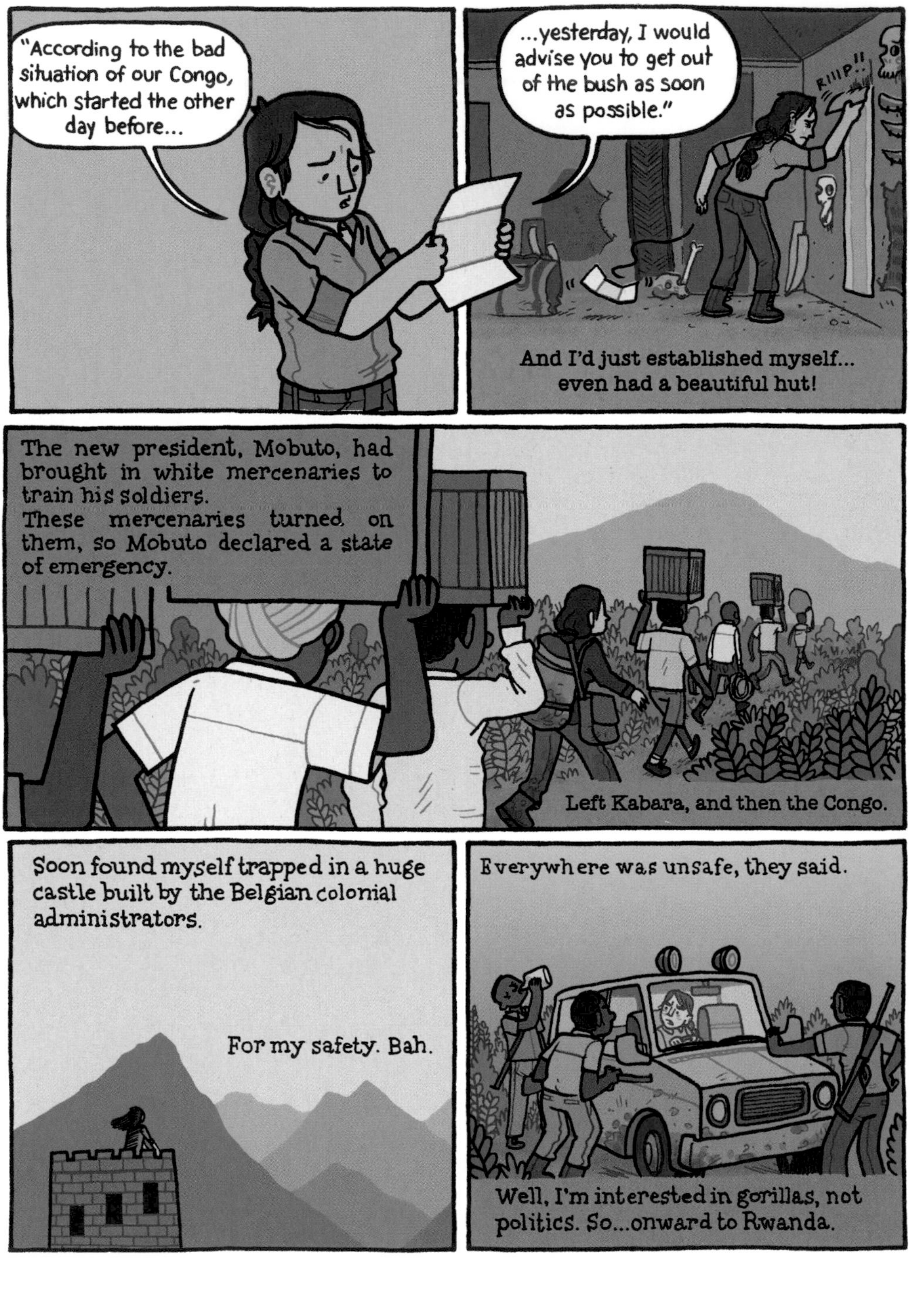
"According to the bad situation of our Congo, which started the other day before...
...yesterday, I would advise you to get out of the bush as soon as possible."
RIIIP!!
And I'd just established myself... even had a beautiful hut!
The new president, Mobuto, had brought in white mercenaries to train his soldiers.
These mercenaries turned on them, so Mobuto declared a state of emergency.
Left Kabara, and then the Congo.
Soon found myself trapped in a huge castle built by the Belgian colonial administrators.
For my safety. Bah.
Everywhere was unsafe, they said.
Well, I'm interested in gorillas, not politics. So...onward to Rwanda.

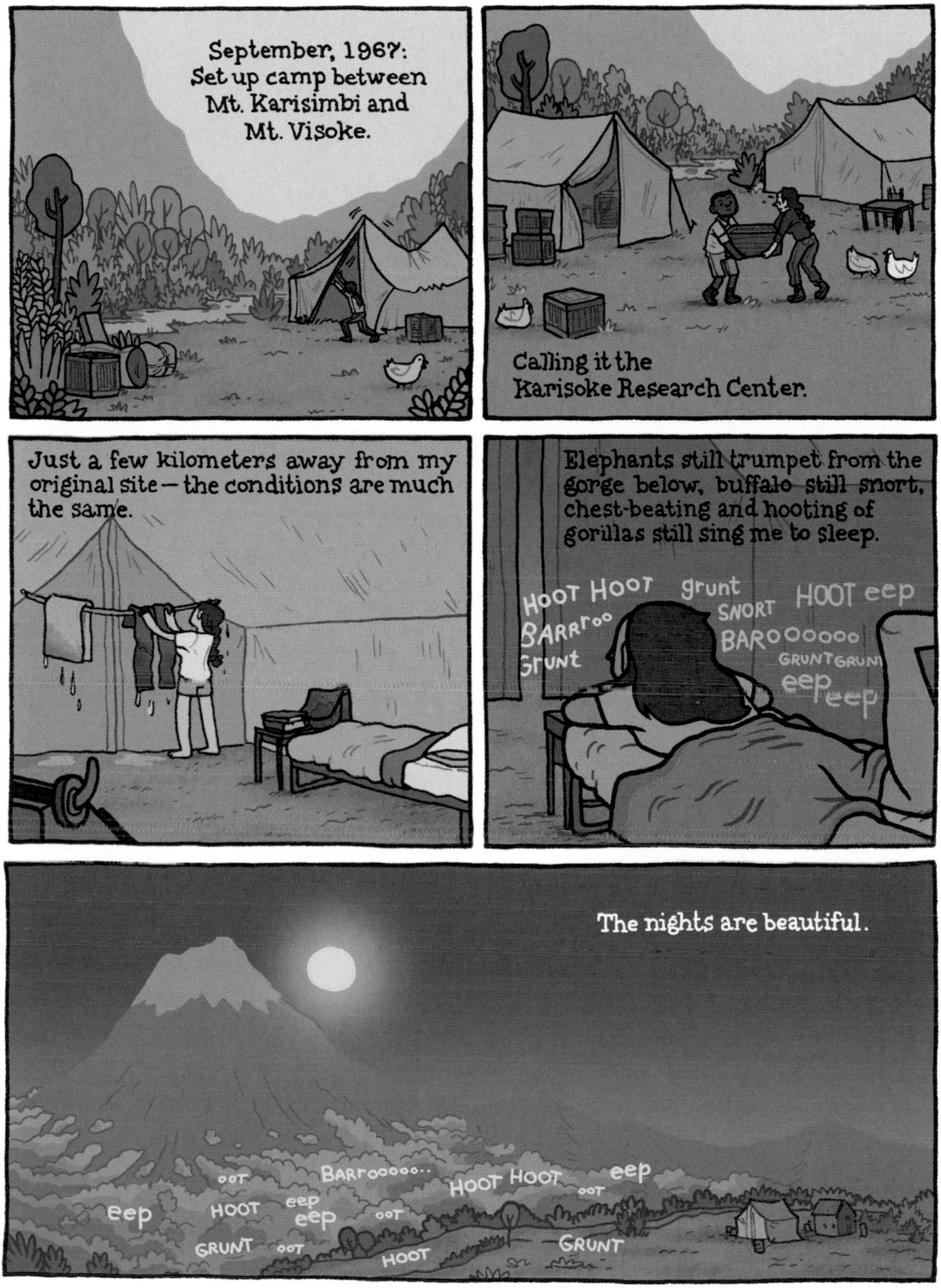
September, 1967: Set up camp between Mt. Karisimbi and Mt. Visoke.
Calling it the Karisoke Research Center.
Just a few kilometers away from my original site — the conditions are much the same.
Elephants still trumpet from the gorge below, buffalo still snort, chest-beating and hooting of gorillas still sing me to sleep.
HOOT HOOT
grunt
HOOT eep
SNORT
BARRroo
BAROOOOOO
Grunt
GRUNTGRUNT
eep eep
The nights are beautiful.
BARroooooo..
oot
HOOT HOOT
eep
oot
eep
HOOT
eep
eep
oot
GRUNT
oot
HOOT
GRUNT

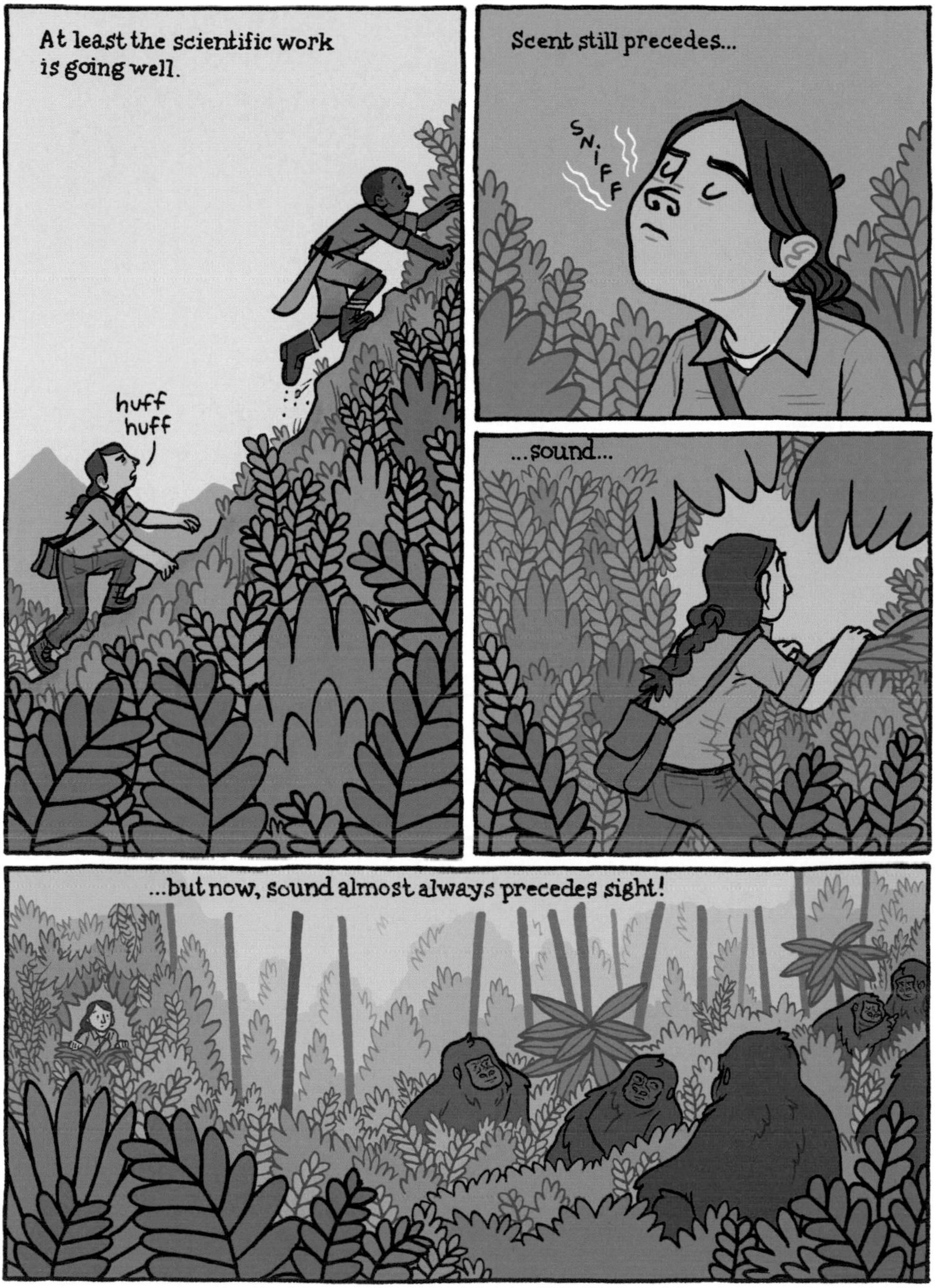
At least the scientific work is going well.
huff huff
Scent still precedes...
SNIFF
...sound...
...but now, sound almost always precedes sight!

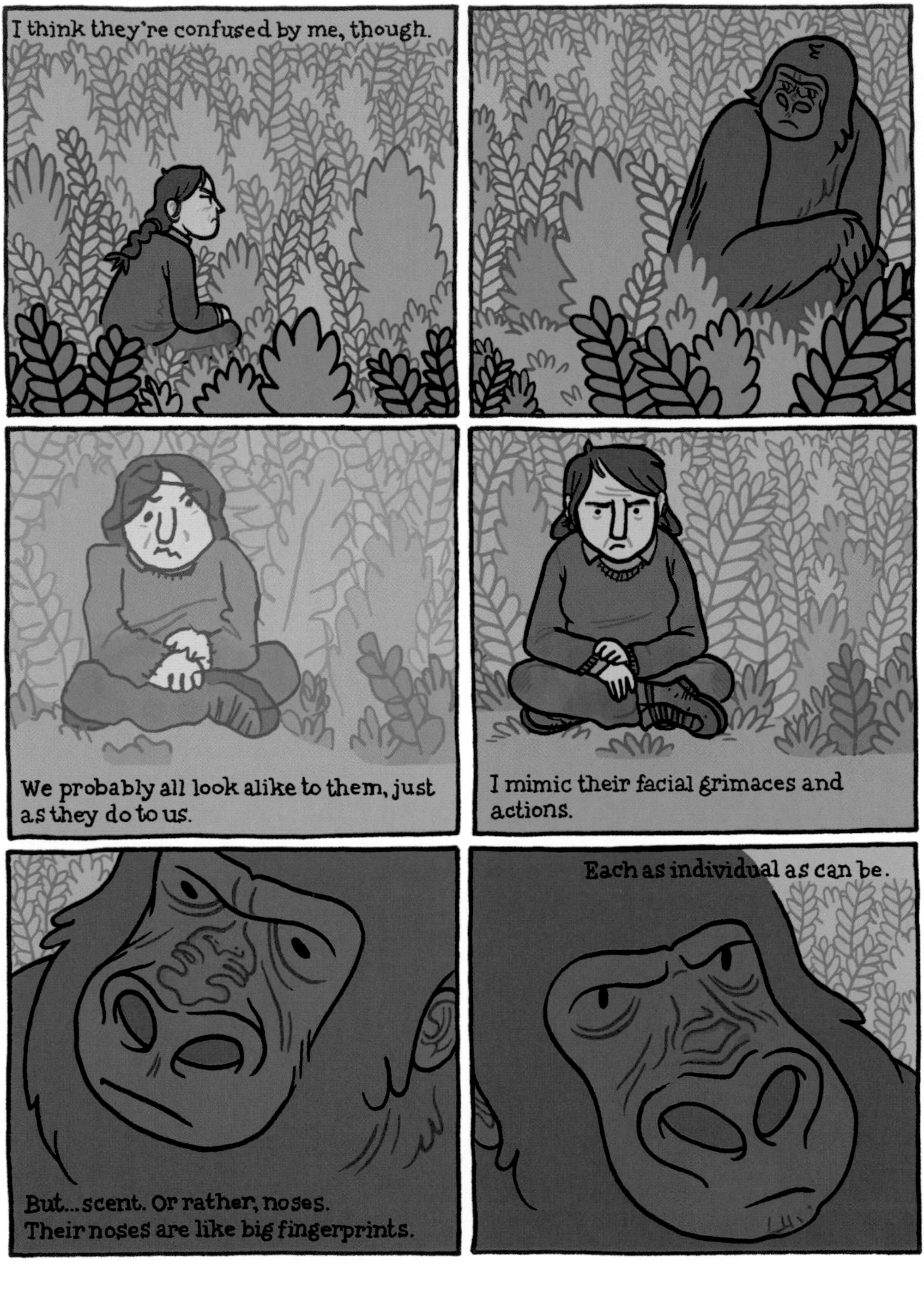
I think they're confused by me, though.
We probably all look alike to them, just as they do to us.
I mimic their facial grimaces and actions.
But...scent. Or rather, noses.
Their noses are like big fingerprints.
Each as individual as can be.

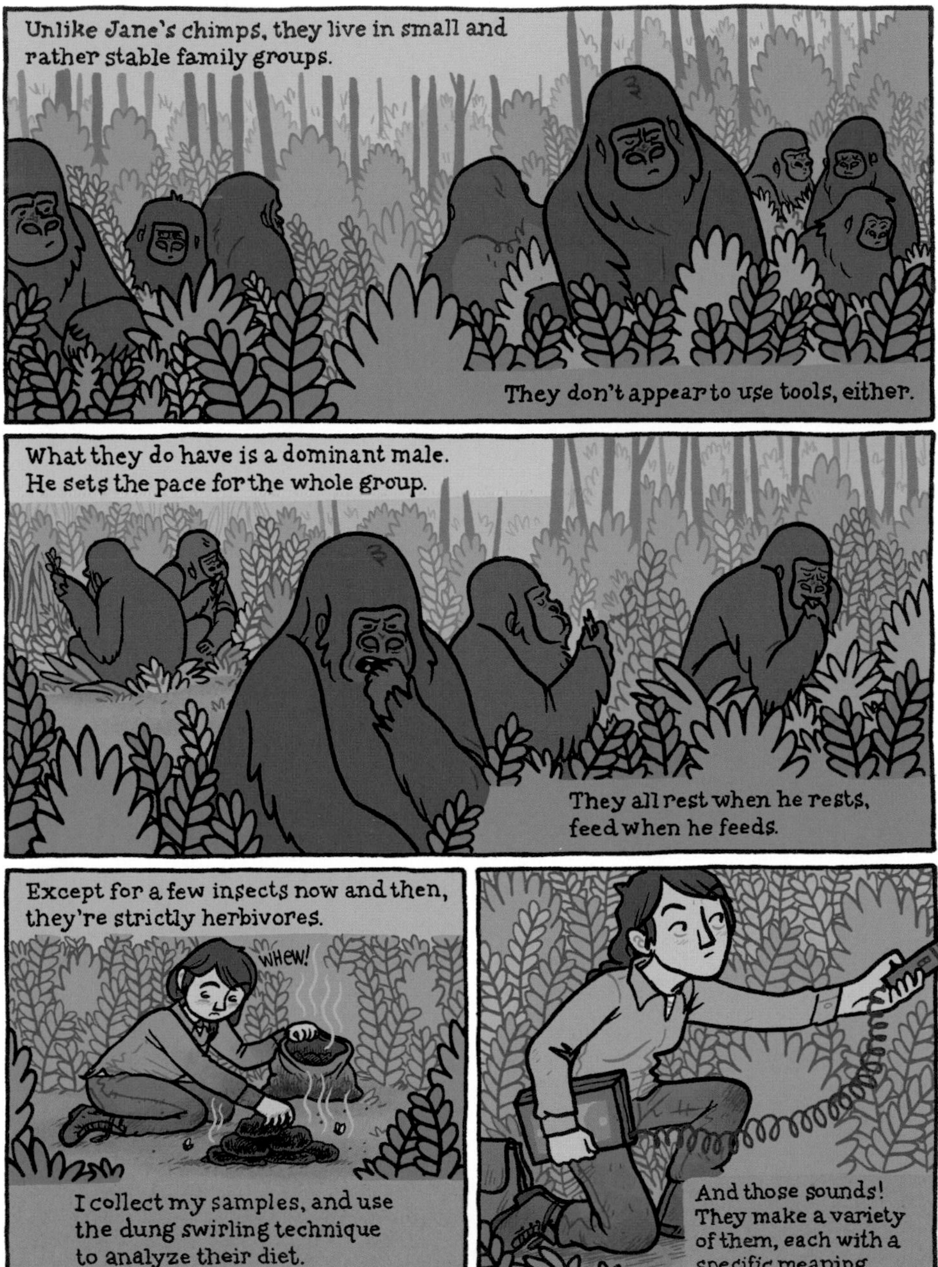
Unlike Jane's chimps, they live in small and rather stable family groups.
They don't appear to use tools, either.
What they do have is a dominant male. He sets the pace for the whole group.
They all rest when he rests, feed when he feeds.
Except for a few insects now and then, they're strictly herbivores.
WHEW!
I collect my samples, and use the dung swirling technique to analyze their diet.
And those sounds! They make a variety of them, each with a specific meaning.

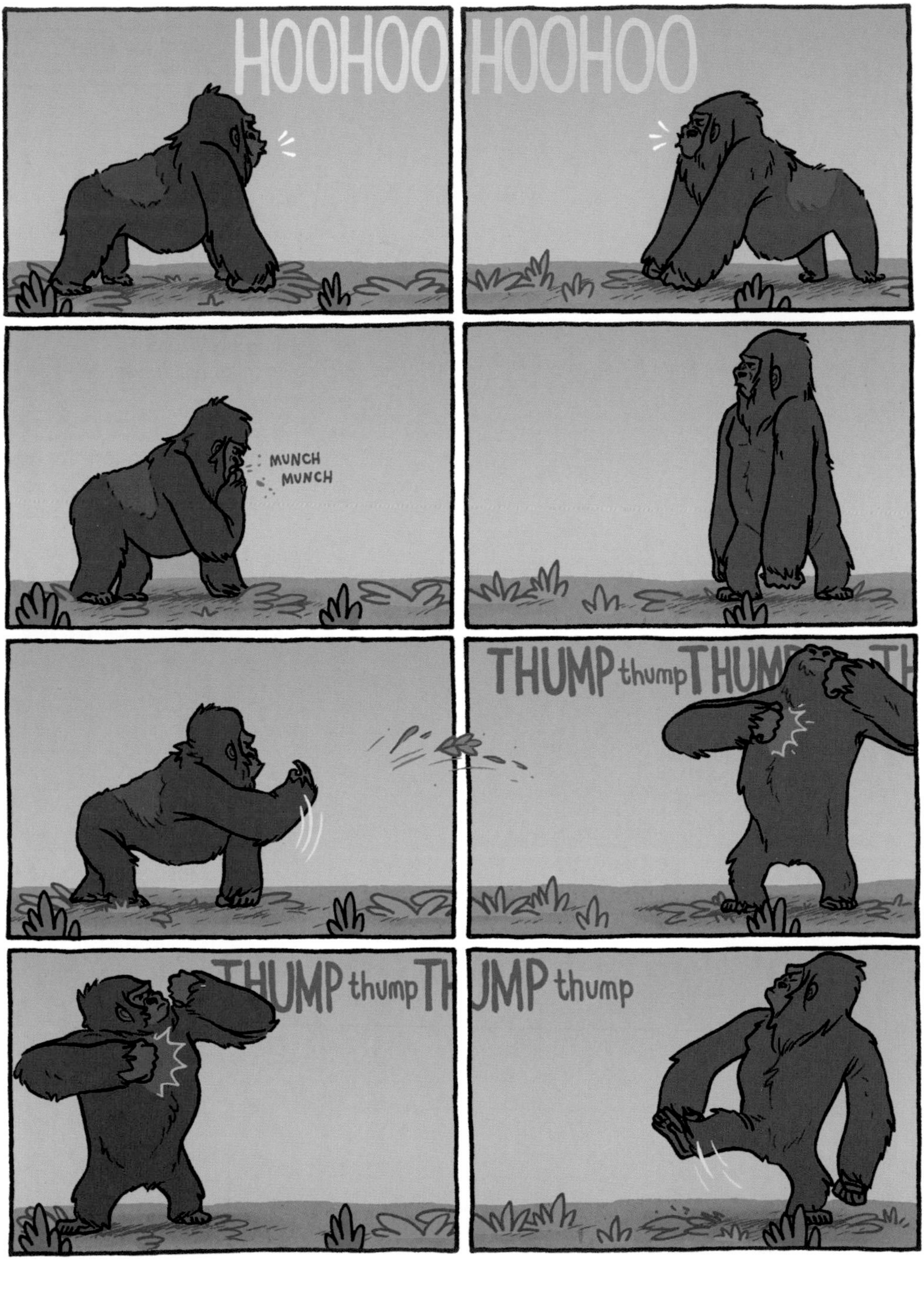
HOOHOO HOOHOO
MUNCH
MUNCH
THUMP thump THUM
THUMP thump THUMP thump

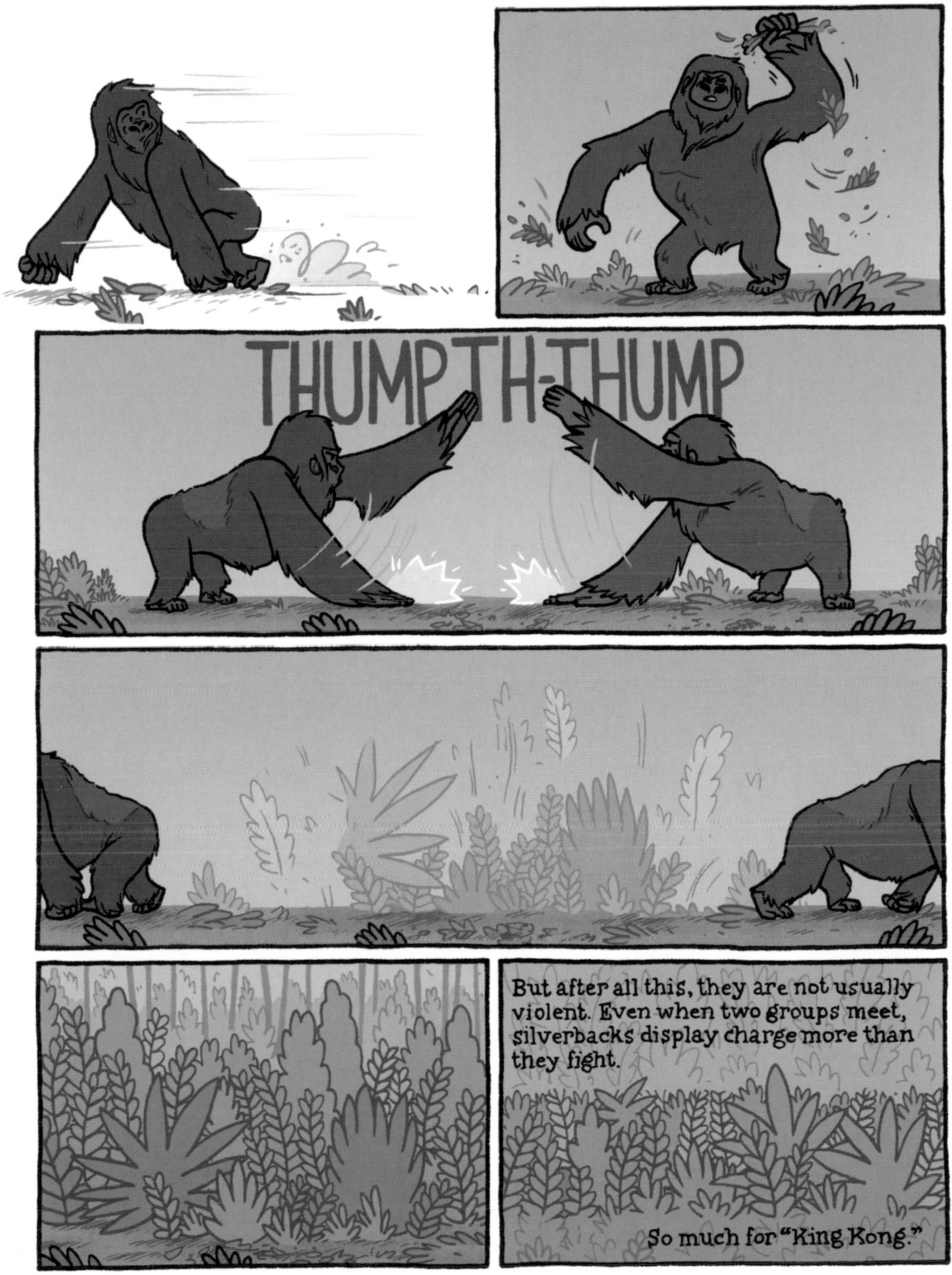
THUMP TH-THUMP
But after all this, they are not usually violent. Even when two groups meet, silverbacks display charge more than they fight.
So much for "King Kong."

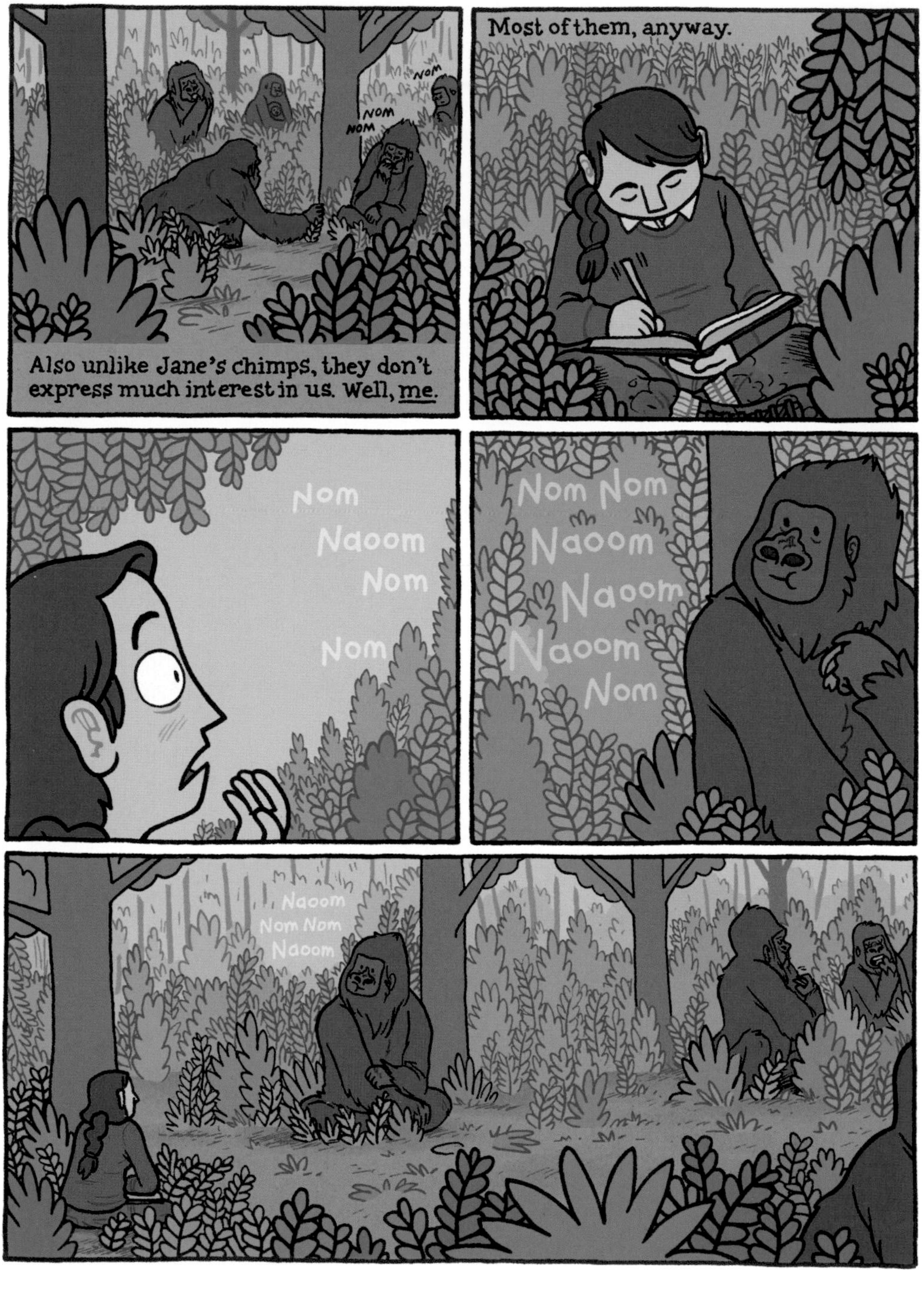
NOM
NOM
NOM
Also unlike Jane's chimps, they don't express much interest in us. Well, me.
Most of them, anyway.
Nom
Naoom
Nom
Nom
Nom Nom
Naoom
Naoom
Naoom
Nom
Naoom
Nom Nom
Naoom

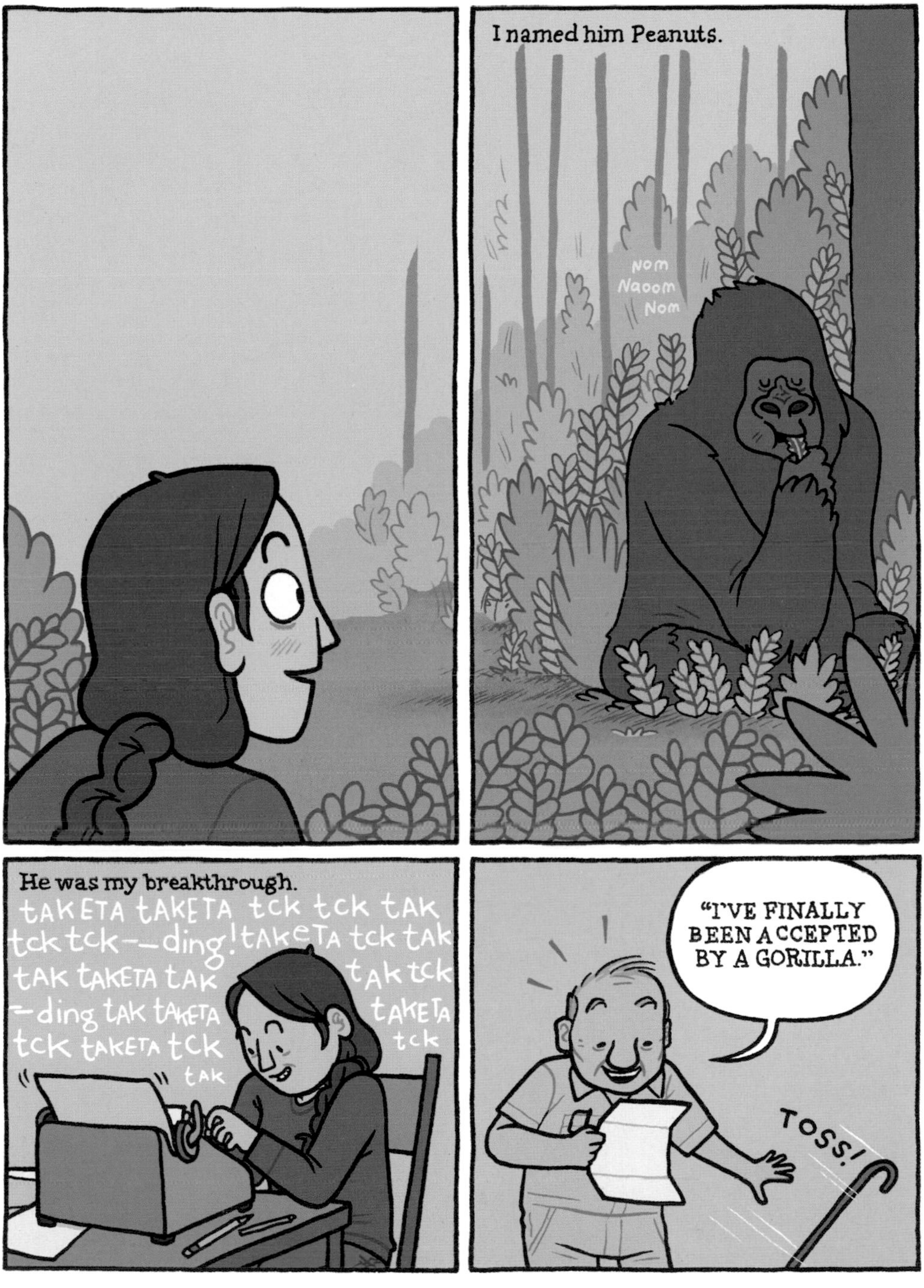

I named him Peanuts.
Nom Naoom Nom
He was my breakthrough.
TAKETA TAKETA tck tck TAK
tck tck—ding! TAKETA tck TAK
TAK TAKETA TAK
—ding TAK TAKETA
tck TAKETA tck
TAK
TAK tck
TAKETA
tck
"I'VE FINALLY BEEN ACCEPTED BY A GORILLA."
TOSS!

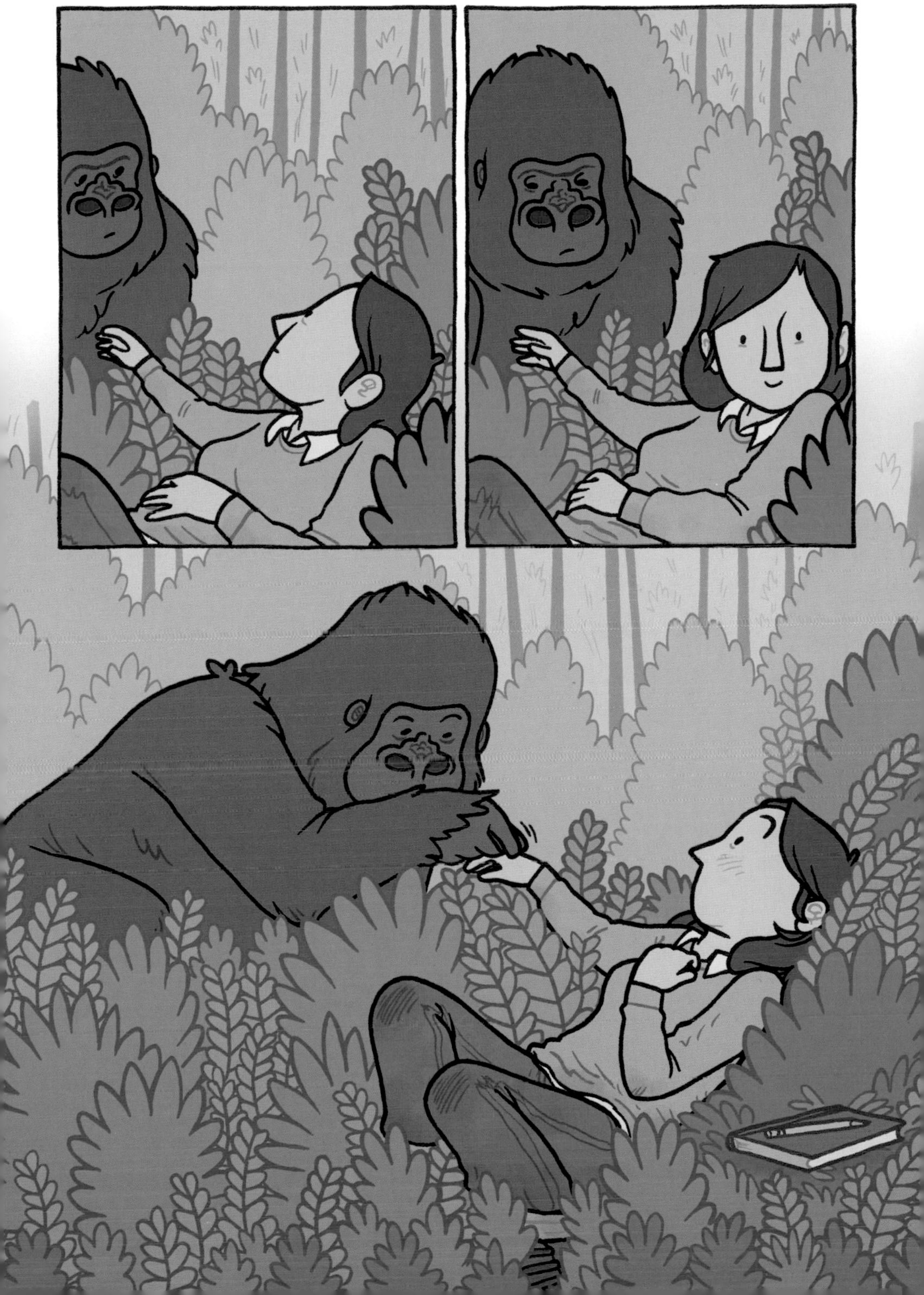

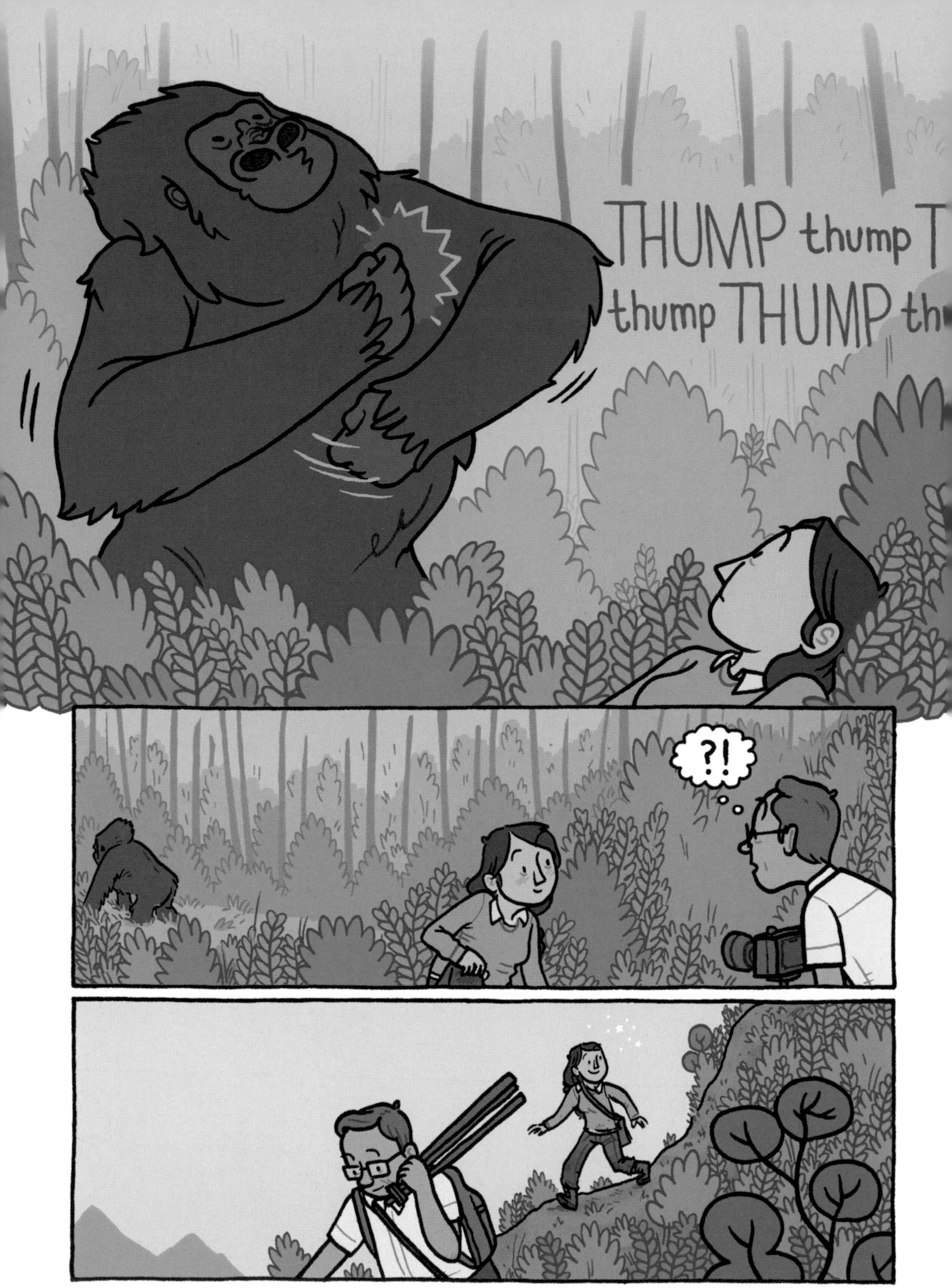
THUMP thump T
thump THUMP th
?!

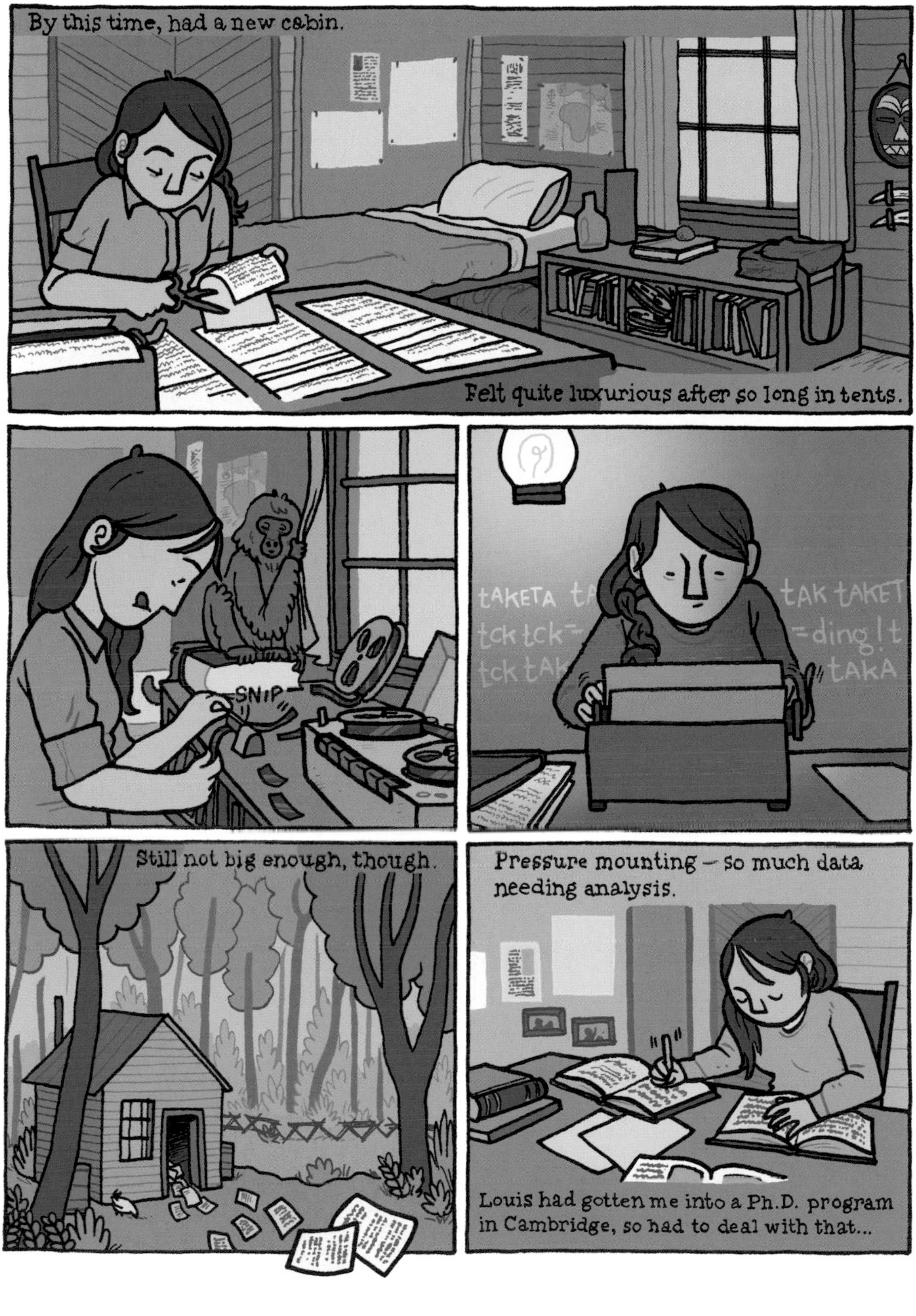
By this time, had a new cabin.
Felt quite luxurious after so long in tents.
SNIP
tAKETA tA
tck tck=
tck tAK
tAK tAKET
=ding! t
tAKA
Still not big enough, though.
Pressure mounting — so much data needing analysis.
Louis had gotten me into a Ph.D. program in Cambridge, so had to deal with that...

And his description of me...

noohoohoohoohoohoohoohoohoo
hoohoohoo
HO
OH
THUMP   HUMPt
thump   ump TH

Said the locals called me "Nyiramachabelli"...

"The old woman who lives alone in the mountains without a man."

Part 3:

WILD PERSON IN THE WOODS

TORONTO
PUBLIC
LIBRARY

IT WASN'T HARD TO CONVINCE ME, REALLY...
I HAD ALWAYS LOVED PRIMATES.

ALL SCIENCES, ACTUALLY. I READ A LOT
ABOUT EVERYTHING. NOT THAT I
UNDERSTOOD EVERYTHING I READ.

FOR INSTANCE, VICTORIAN SCIENTISTS.

THEY WOULD
STUDY ANIMALS...

...METICULOUSLY DESCRIBE THEM...

...AND THEN *KILL THEM* AND BRING THEM HOME.

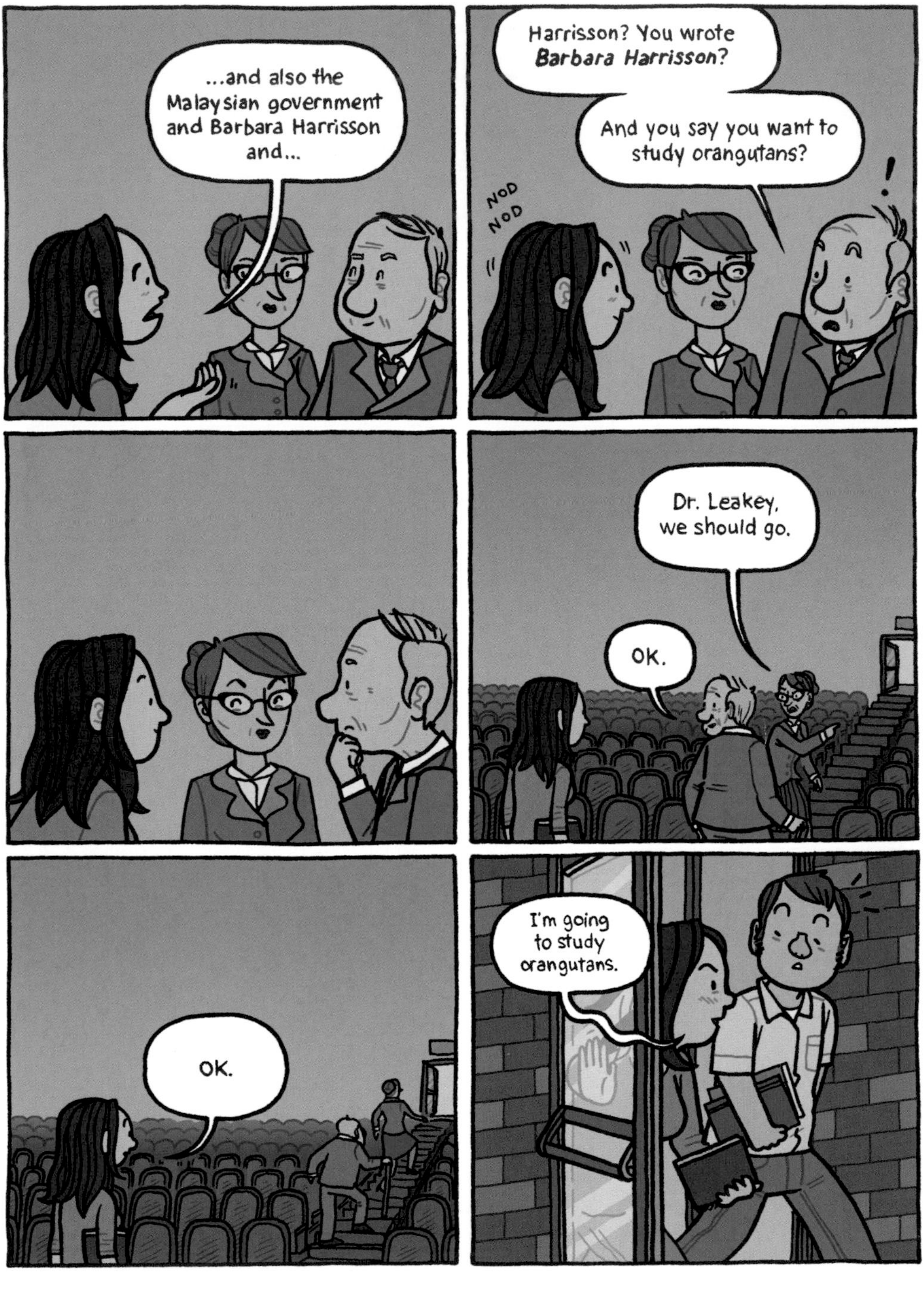
...and also the Malaysian government and Barbara Harrisson and...
Harrisson? You wrote *Barbara Harrisson*?
And you say you want to study orangutans?
NOD NOD
!
Dr. Leakey, we should go.
OK.
OK.
I'm going to study orangutans.

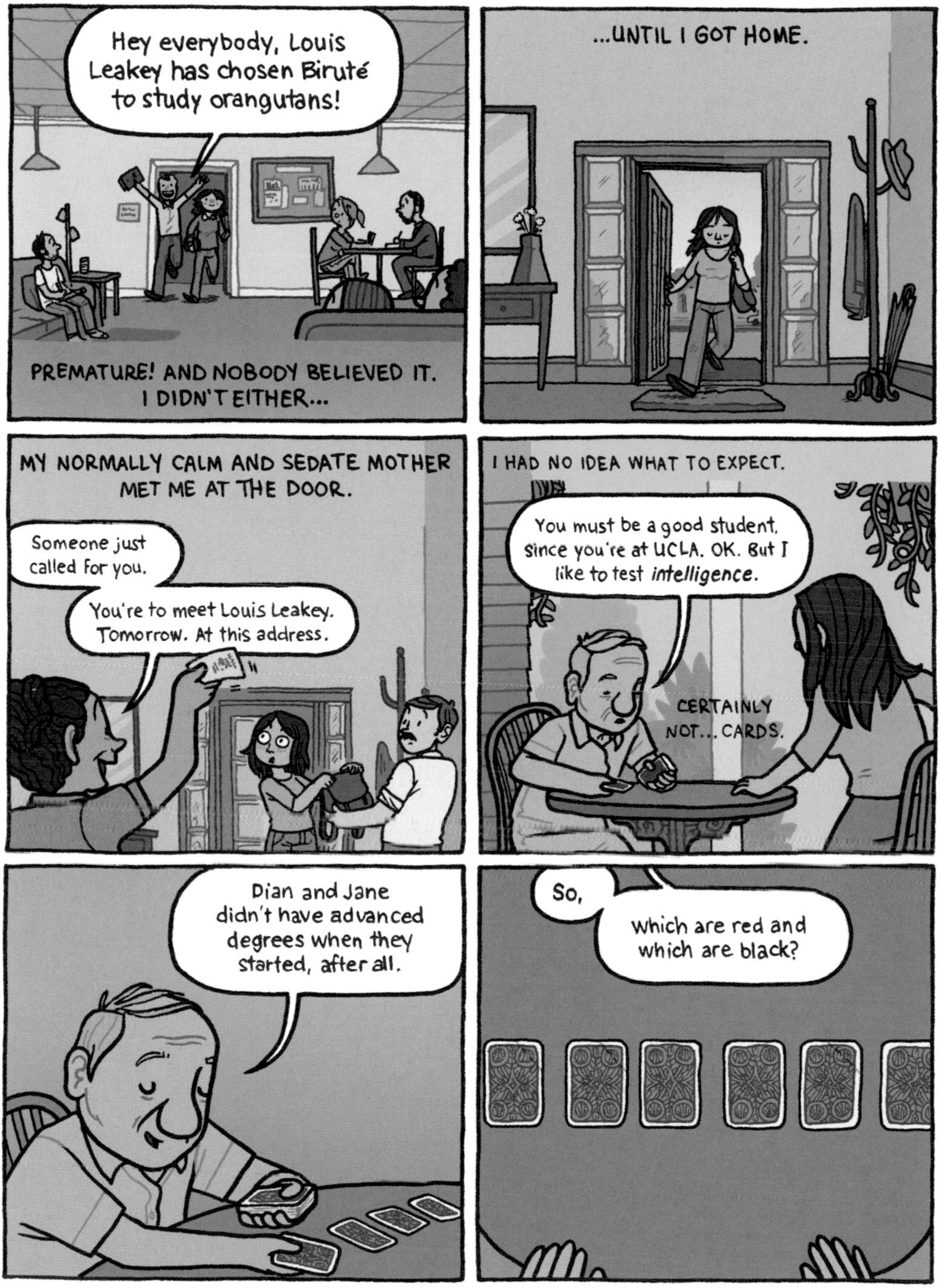
Hey everybody, Louis Leakey has chosen Biruté to study orangutans!
PREMATURE! AND NOBODY BELIEVED IT. I DIDN'T EITHER...
...UNTIL I GOT HOME.
MY NORMALLY CALM AND SEDATE MOTHER MET ME AT THE DOOR.
Someone just called for you.
You're to meet Louis Leakey. Tomorrow. At this address.
I HAD NO IDEA WHAT TO EXPECT.
You must be a good student, since you're at UCLA. OK. But I like to test *intelligence*.
CERTAINLY NOT... CARDS.
Dian and Jane didn't have advanced degrees when they started, after all.
So,
Which are red and which are black?

88

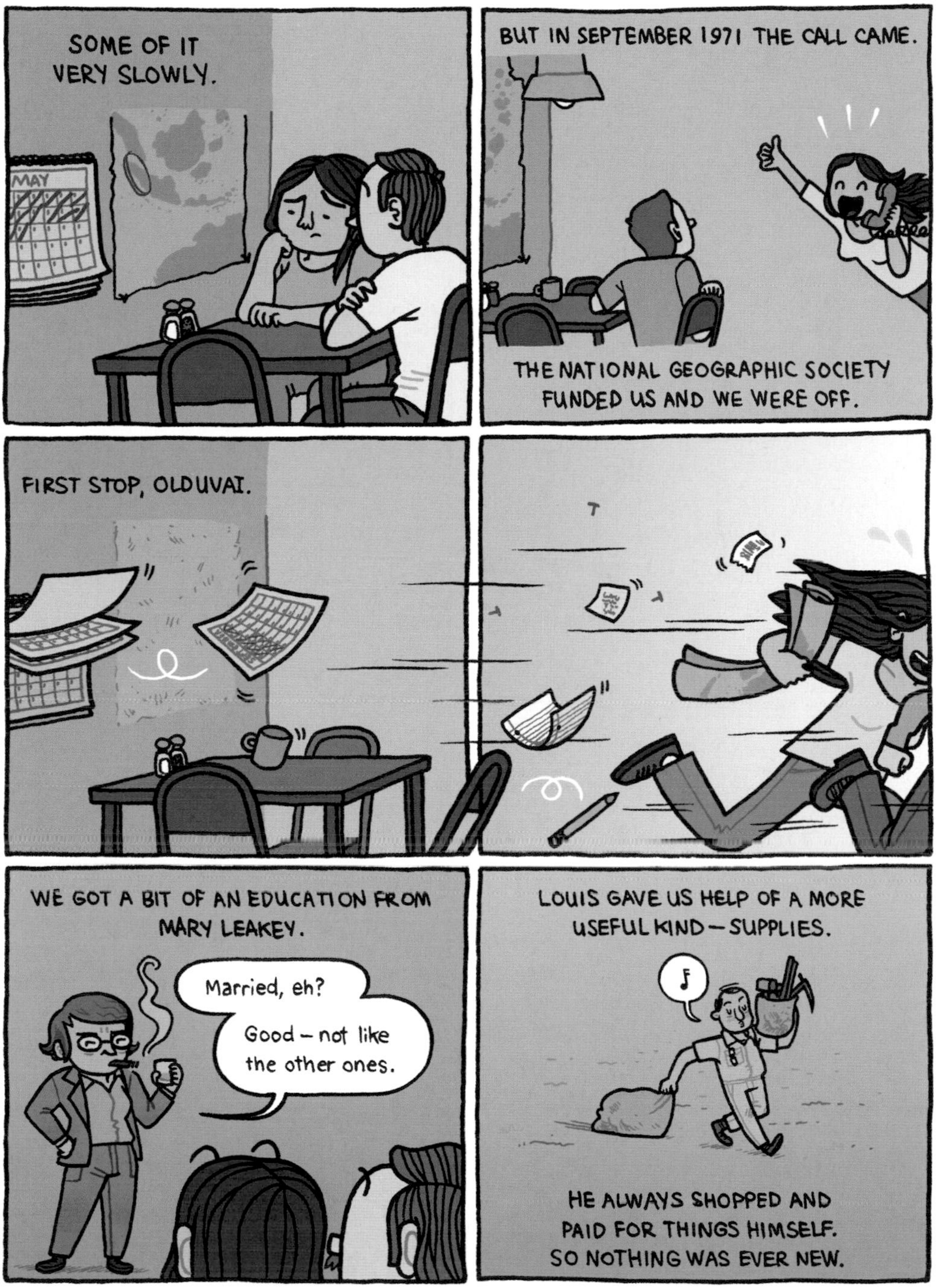
SOME OF IT VERY SLOWLY.
MAY
BUT IN SEPTEMBER 1971 THE CALL CAME.
THE NATIONAL GEOGRAPHIC SOCIETY FUNDED US AND WE WERE OFF.
FIRST STOP, OLDUVAI.
WE GOT A BIT OF AN EDUCATION FROM MARY LEAKEY.
Married, eh?
Good – not like the other ones.
LOUIS GAVE US HELP OF A MORE USEFUL KIND – SUPPLIES.
HE ALWAYS SHOPPED AND PAID FOR THINGS HIMSELF. SO NOTHING WAS EVER NEW.

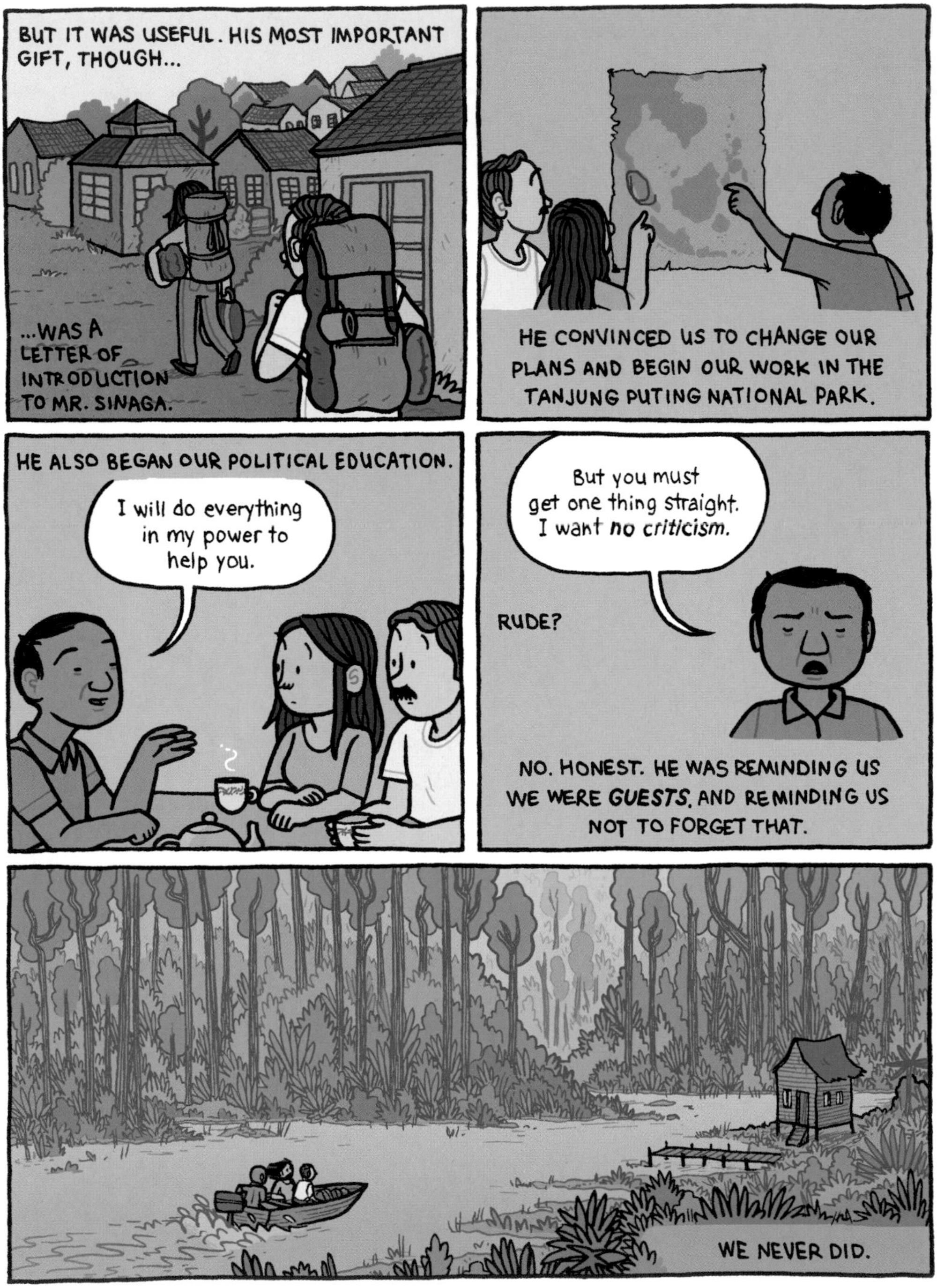
BUT IT WAS USEFUL. HIS MOST IMPORTANT GIFT, THOUGH...
...WAS A LETTER OF INTRODUCTION TO MR. SINAGA.
HE CONVINCED US TO CHANGE OUR PLANS AND BEGIN OUR WORK IN THE TANJUNG PUTING NATIONAL PARK.
HE ALSO BEGAN OUR POLITICAL EDUCATION.
I will do everything in my power to help you.
But you must get one thing straight. I want *no criticism.*
RUDE?
NO. HONEST. HE WAS REMINDING US WE WERE *GUESTS*, AND REMINDING US NOT TO FORGET THAT.
WE NEVER DID.

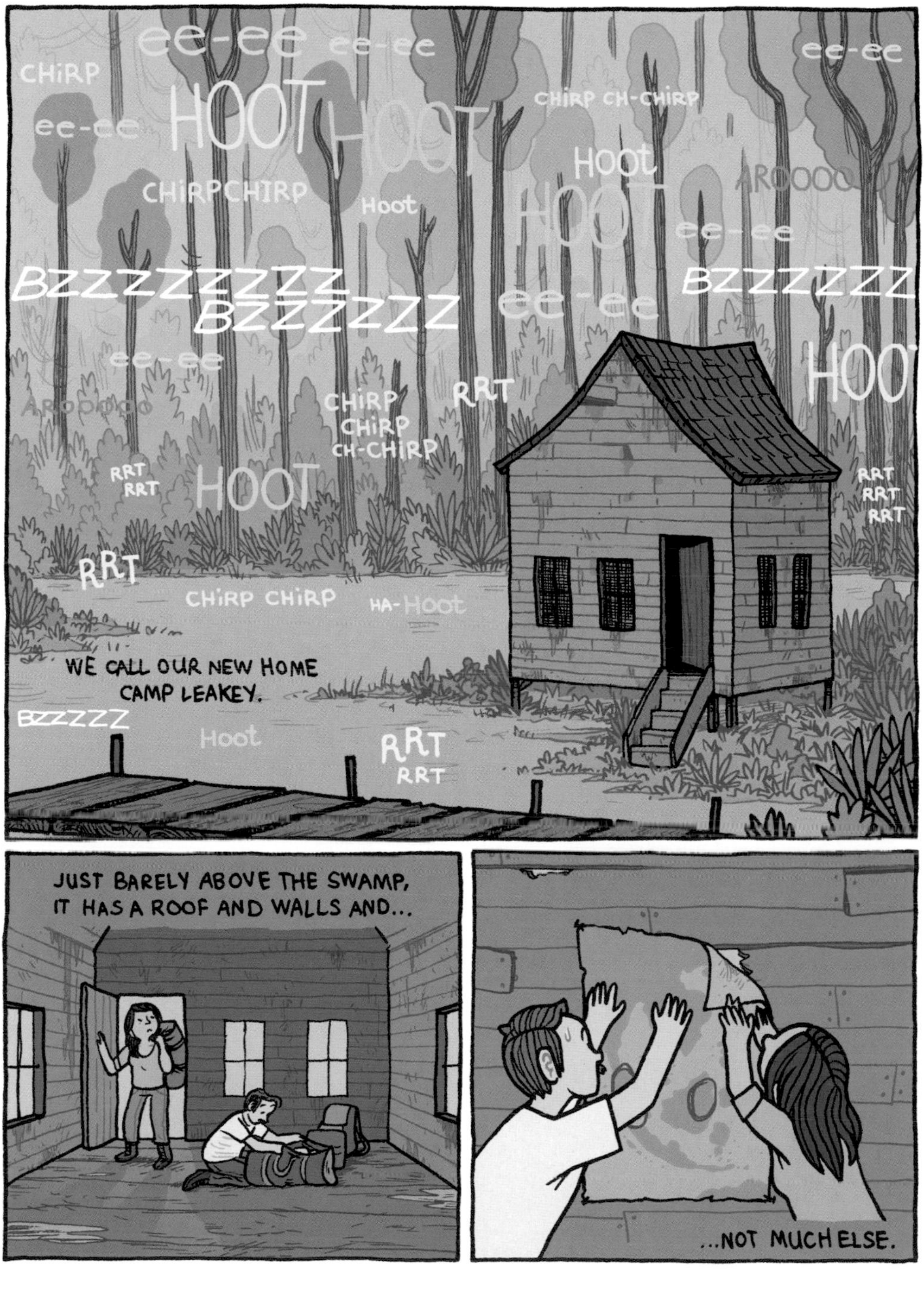
ee-ee ee-ee
ee-ee
CHiRP
HOOT HOOT
CHIRP CH-CHIRP
ee-ee
HOOT
CHiRPCHIRP
Hoot
HOOT
AROOOO
ee-ee
BZZZZZZZZ
BZZZZZZ
ee-ee
BZZZZZZ
ee-ee
HOOT
AROOOO
CHiRP
CHiRP
CH-CHIRP
RRT
RRT
RRT
HOOT
RRT
RRT
RRT
RRT
CHiRP CHiRP
HA-Hoot
WE CALL OUR NEW HOME CAMP LEAKEY.
BZZZZZ
Hoot
RRT
RRT
JUST BARELY ABOVE THE SWAMP, IT HAS A ROOF AND WALLS AND...
...NOT MUCH ELSE.

MY WALK TO WORK COULDN'T BE MORE DIFFERENT THAN IN LOS ANGELES.

BZZZZZZZZzz
HOOT
HOOT
eeeeeeee
CHIRP CHIRP
CHIRP CHIRP
CHIRP CHIRP
BZZZZ
RRT
HOOT
oaaiieeerr
RRT
RRT
CHIRP
BZZZZZZZZ
BZZZZ ZZZ
CHIRP

EXCEPT FOR THE NOISE. THE JUNGLE IS AS LOUD AS A BUSY L.A. STREET CORNER.

AND THE ORANGUTANS—

—THAT'S ALSO THE SAME.

MEANING, JUST LIKE IN L.A., I DON'T SEE ANY.

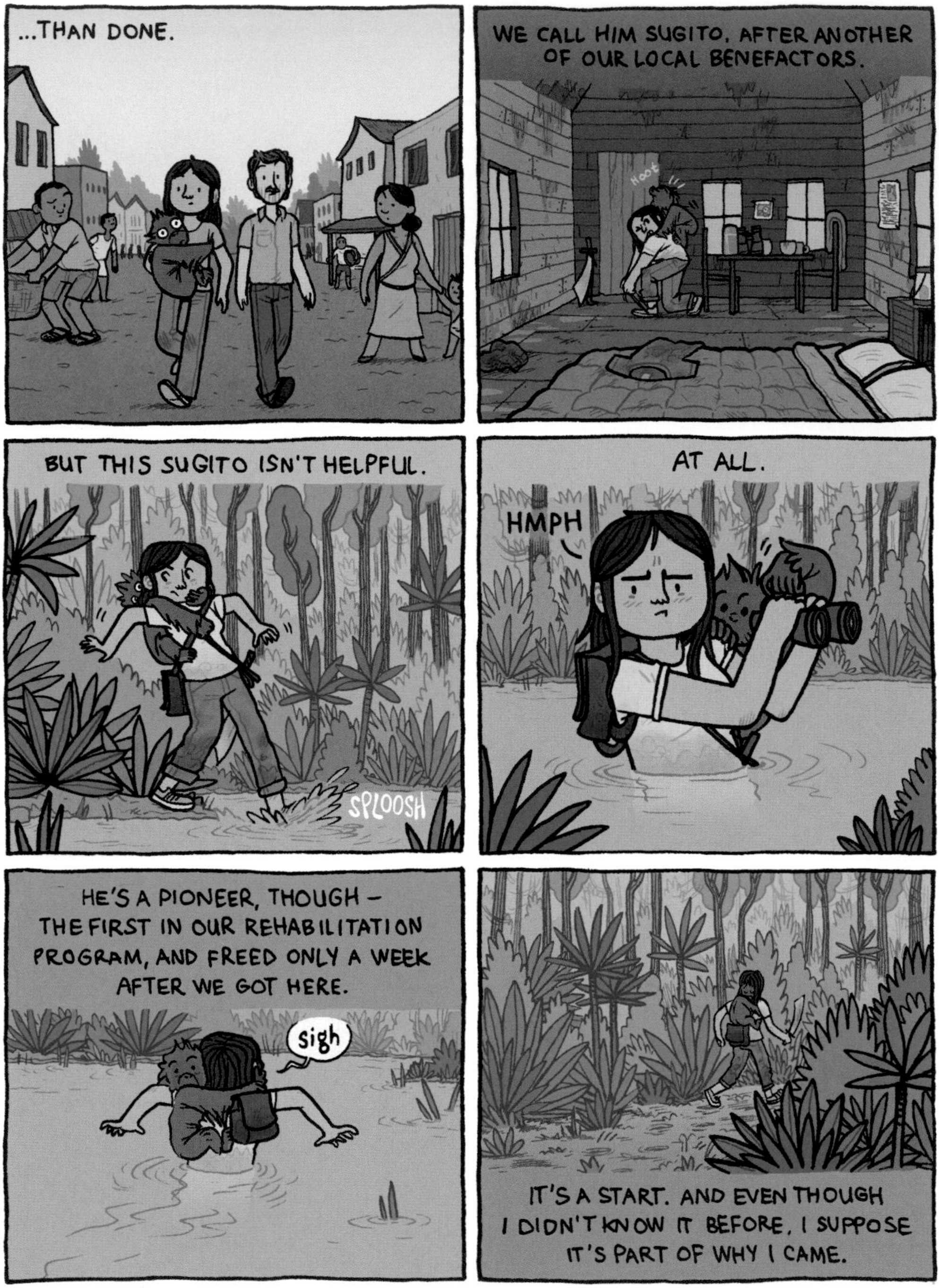
...THAN DONE.
WE CALL HIM SUGITO, AFTER ANOTHER OF OUR LOCAL BENEFACTORS.
Hoot
BUT THIS SUGITO ISN'T HELPFUL.
SPLOOSH
AT ALL.
HMPH
HE'S A PIONEER, THOUGH – THE FIRST IN OUR REHABILITATION PROGRAM, AND FREED ONLY A WEEK AFTER WE GOT HERE.
sigh
IT'S A START. AND EVEN THOUGH I DIDN'T KNOW IT BEFORE, I SUPPOSE IT'S PART OF WHY I CAME.

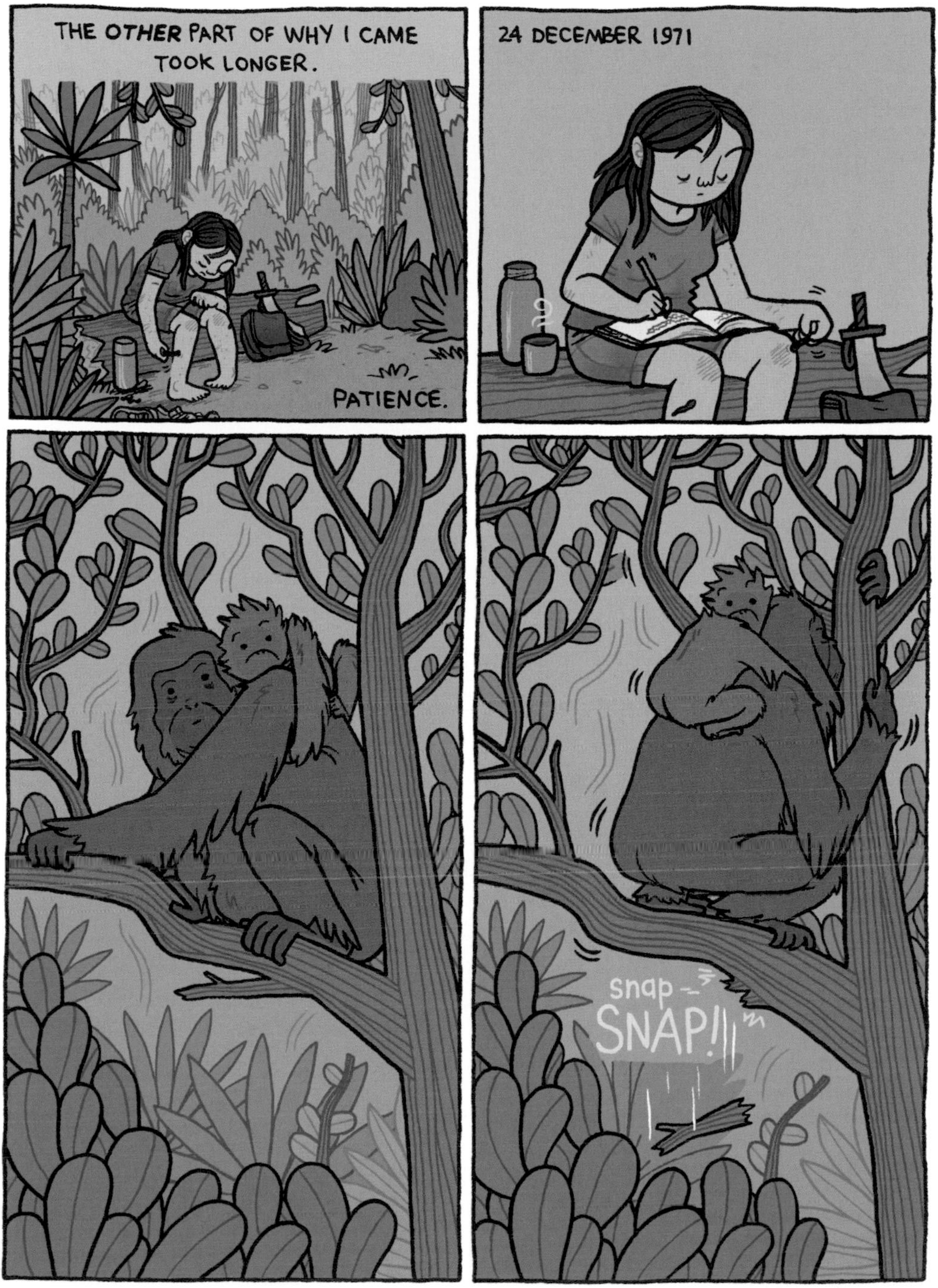
THE *OTHER* PART OF WHY I CAME TOOK LONGER.
PATIENCE.
24 DECEMBER 1971
snap
SNAP!

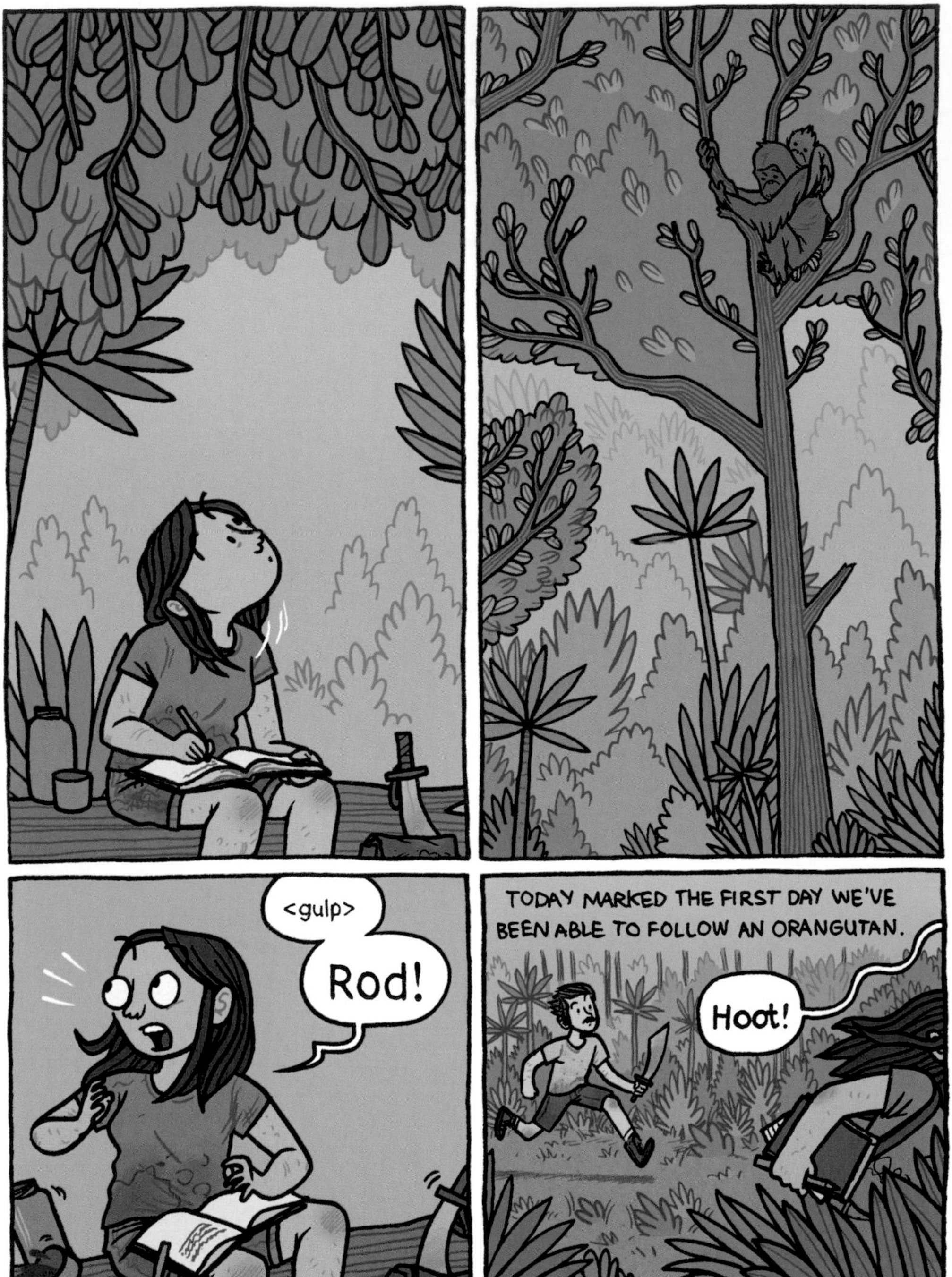
<gulp>
Rod!
TODAY MARKED THE FIRST DAY WE'VE BEEN ABLE TO FOLLOW AN ORANGUTAN.
Hoot!

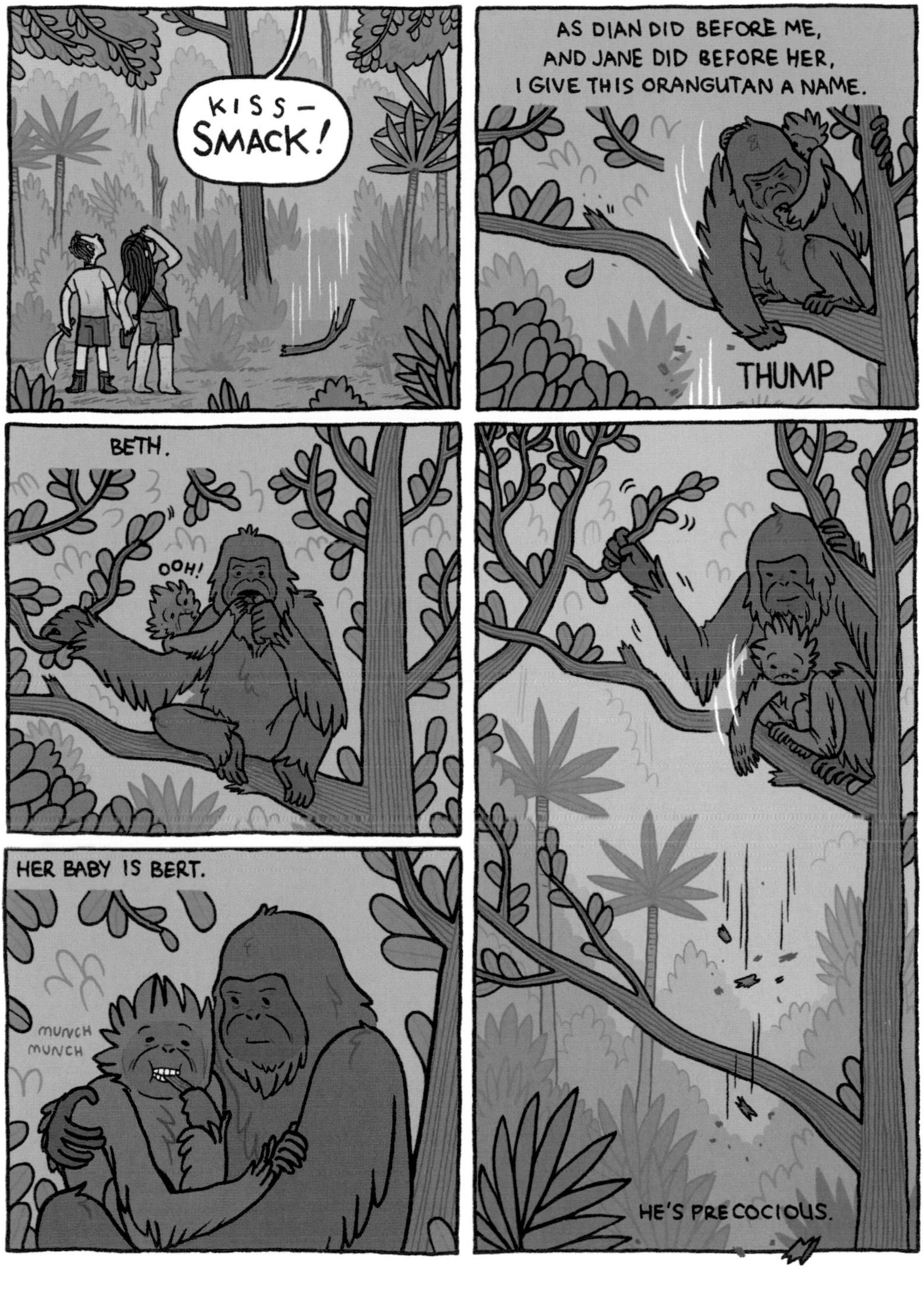

KISS-SMACK!
AS DIAN DID BEFORE ME, AND JANE DID BEFORE HER, I GIVE THIS ORANGUTAN A NAME.
THUMP
BETH.
OOH!
HER BABY IS BERT.
MUNCH MUNCH
HE'S PRECOCIOUS.

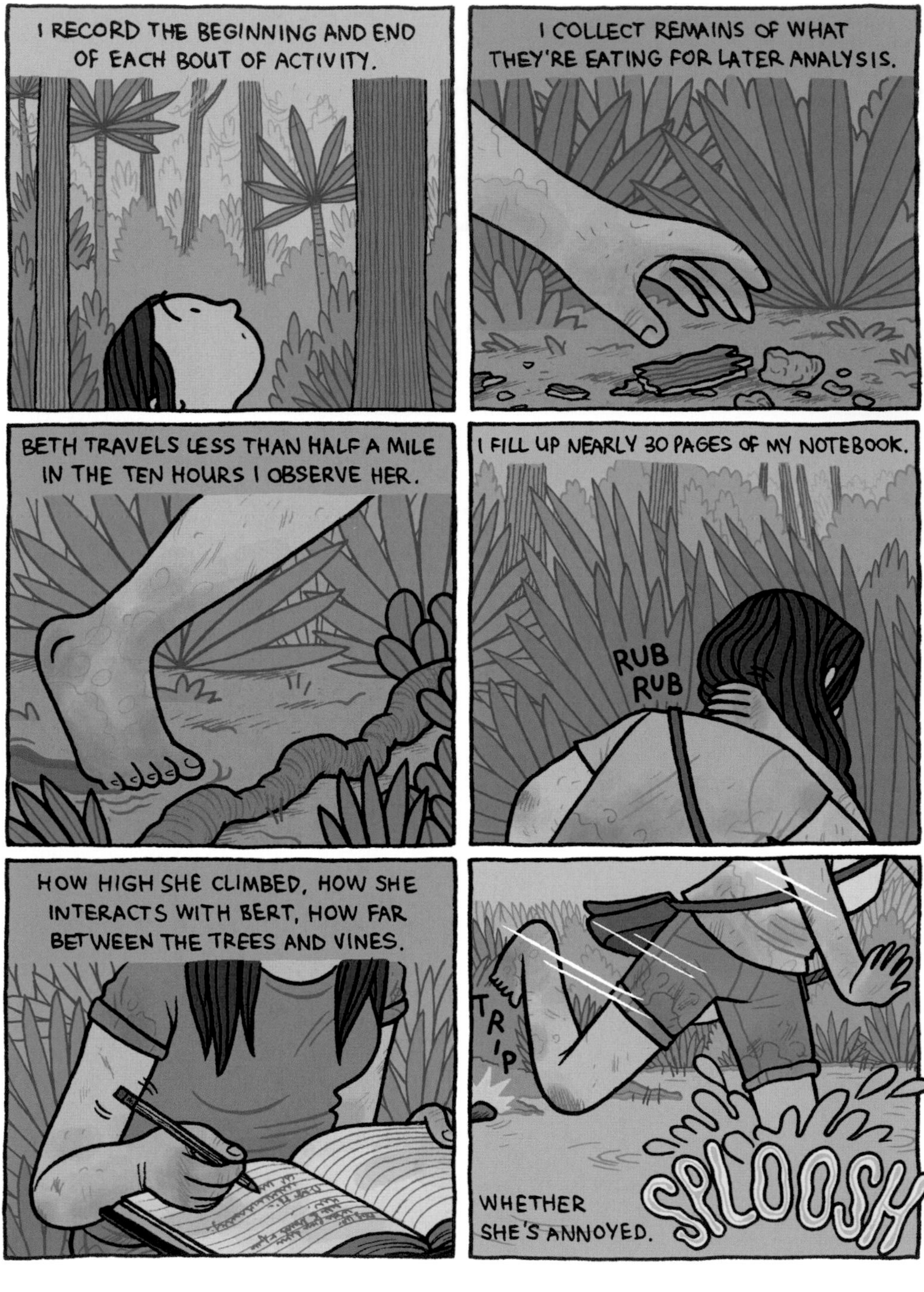
I RECORD THE BEGINNING AND END OF EACH BOUT OF ACTIVITY.
I COLLECT REMAINS OF WHAT THEY'RE EATING FOR LATER ANALYSIS.
BETH TRAVELS LESS THAN HALF A MILE IN THE TEN HOURS I OBSERVE HER.
I FILL UP NEARLY 30 PAGES OF MY NOTEBOOK.
RUB RUB
HOW HIGH SHE CLIMBED, HOW SHE INTERACTS WITH BERT, HOW FAR BETWEEN THE TREES AND VINES.
TRIP
WHETHER SHE'S ANNOYED.
SPLOOSH

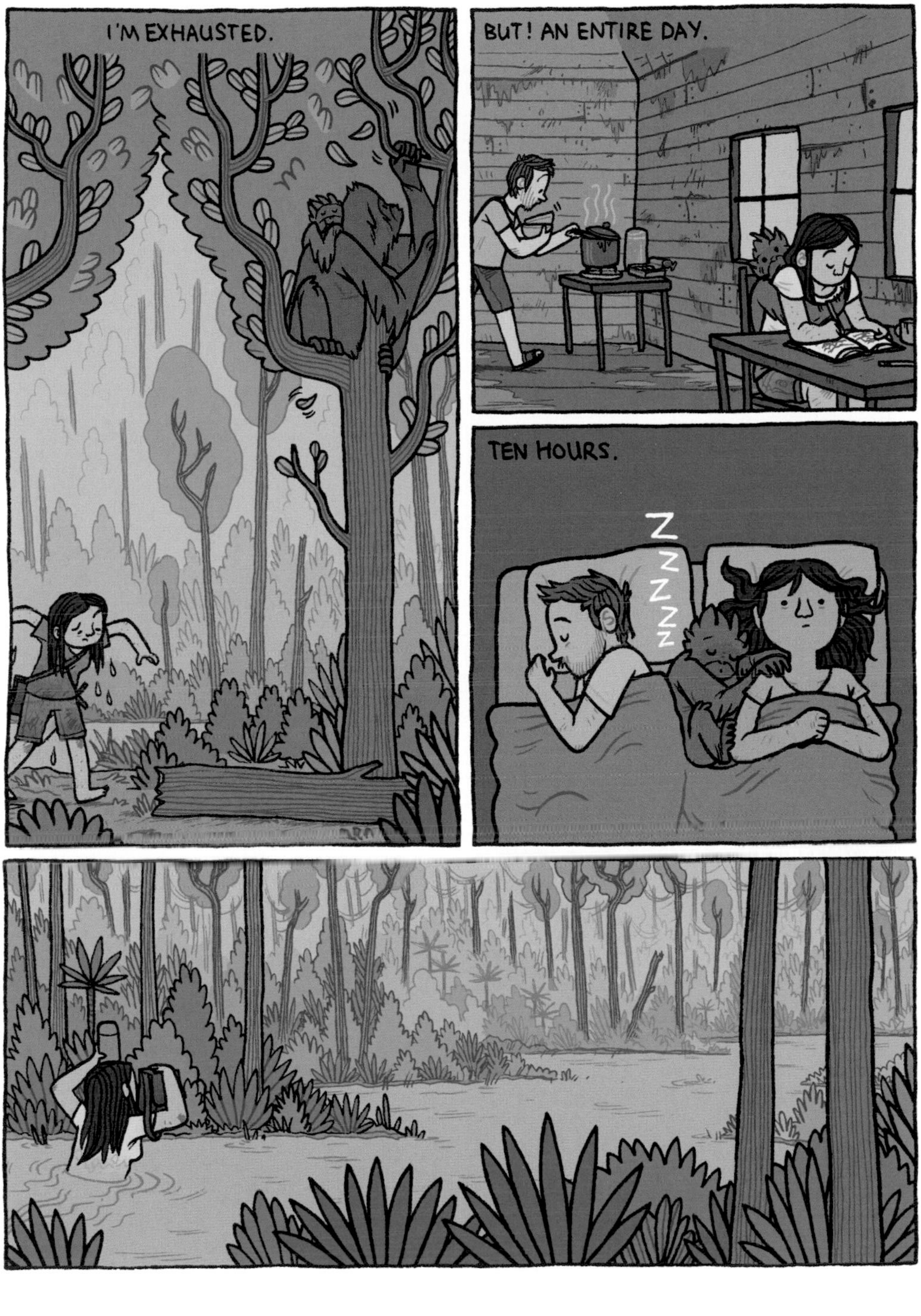
I'M EXHAUSTED.
BUT! AN ENTIRE DAY.
TEN HOURS.
ZZZZZ

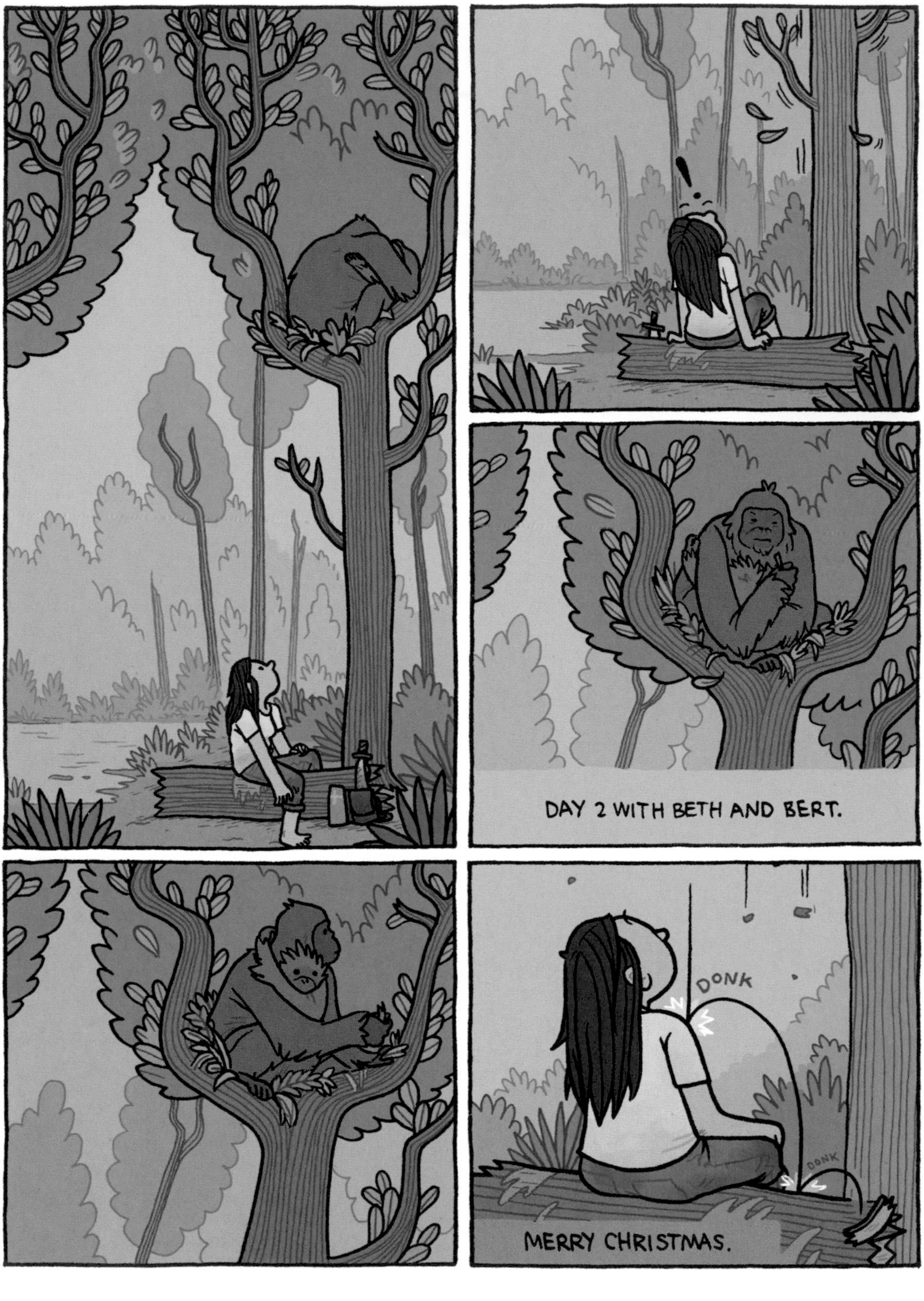
!
DAY 2 WITH BETH AND BERT.
DONK
DONK
MERRY CHRISTMAS.

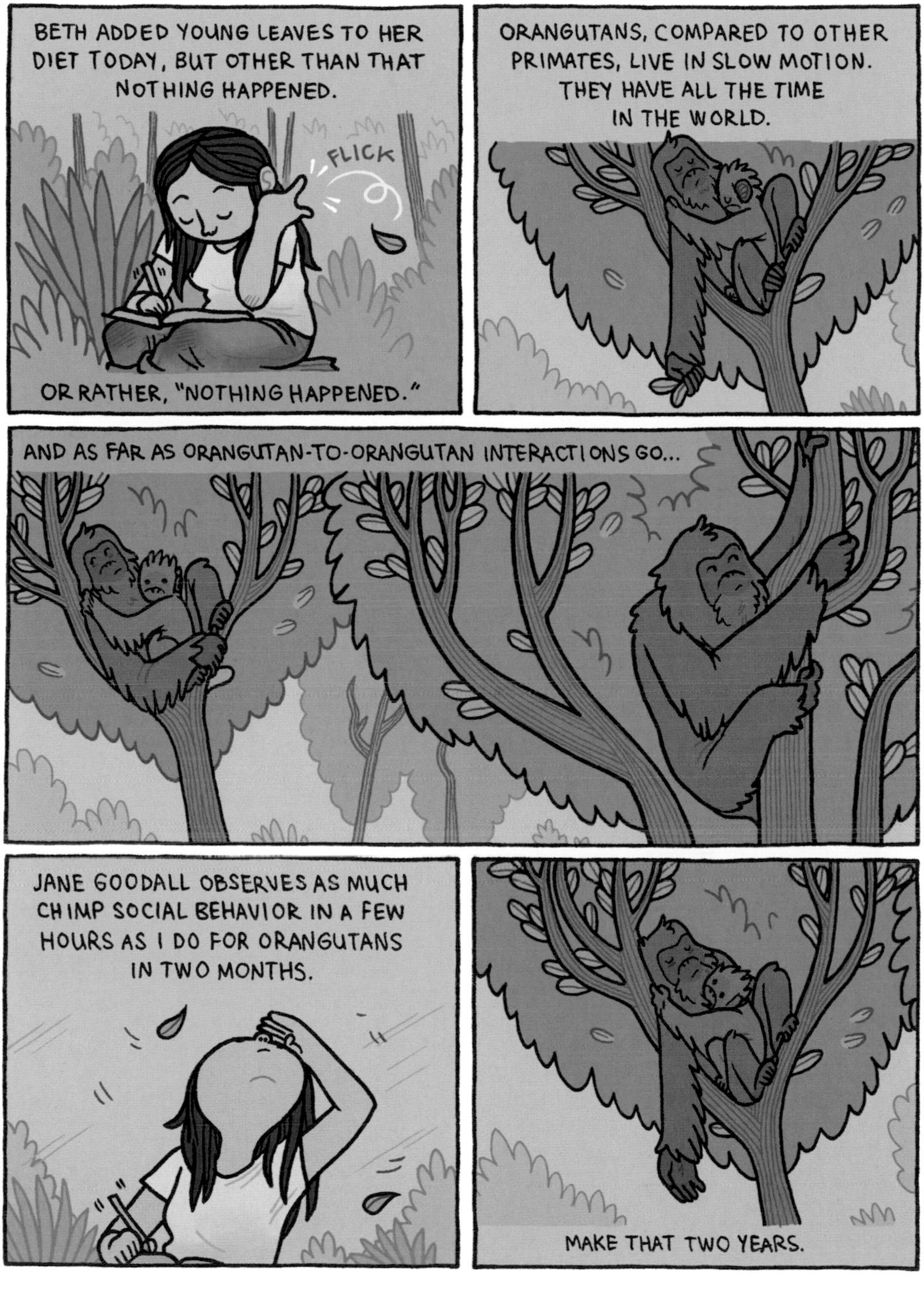
BETH ADDED YOUNG LEAVES TO HER DIET TODAY, BUT OTHER THAN THAT NOTHING HAPPENED.
FLICK
OR RATHER, "NOTHING HAPPENED."
ORANGUTANS, COMPARED TO OTHER PRIMATES, LIVE IN SLOW MOTION. THEY HAVE ALL THE TIME IN THE WORLD.
AND AS FAR AS ORANGUTAN-TO-ORANGUTAN INTERACTIONS GO...
JANE GOODALL OBSERVES AS MUCH CHIMP SOCIAL BEHAVIOR IN A FEW HOURS AS I DO FOR ORANGUTANS IN TWO MONTHS.
MAKE THAT TWO YEARS.

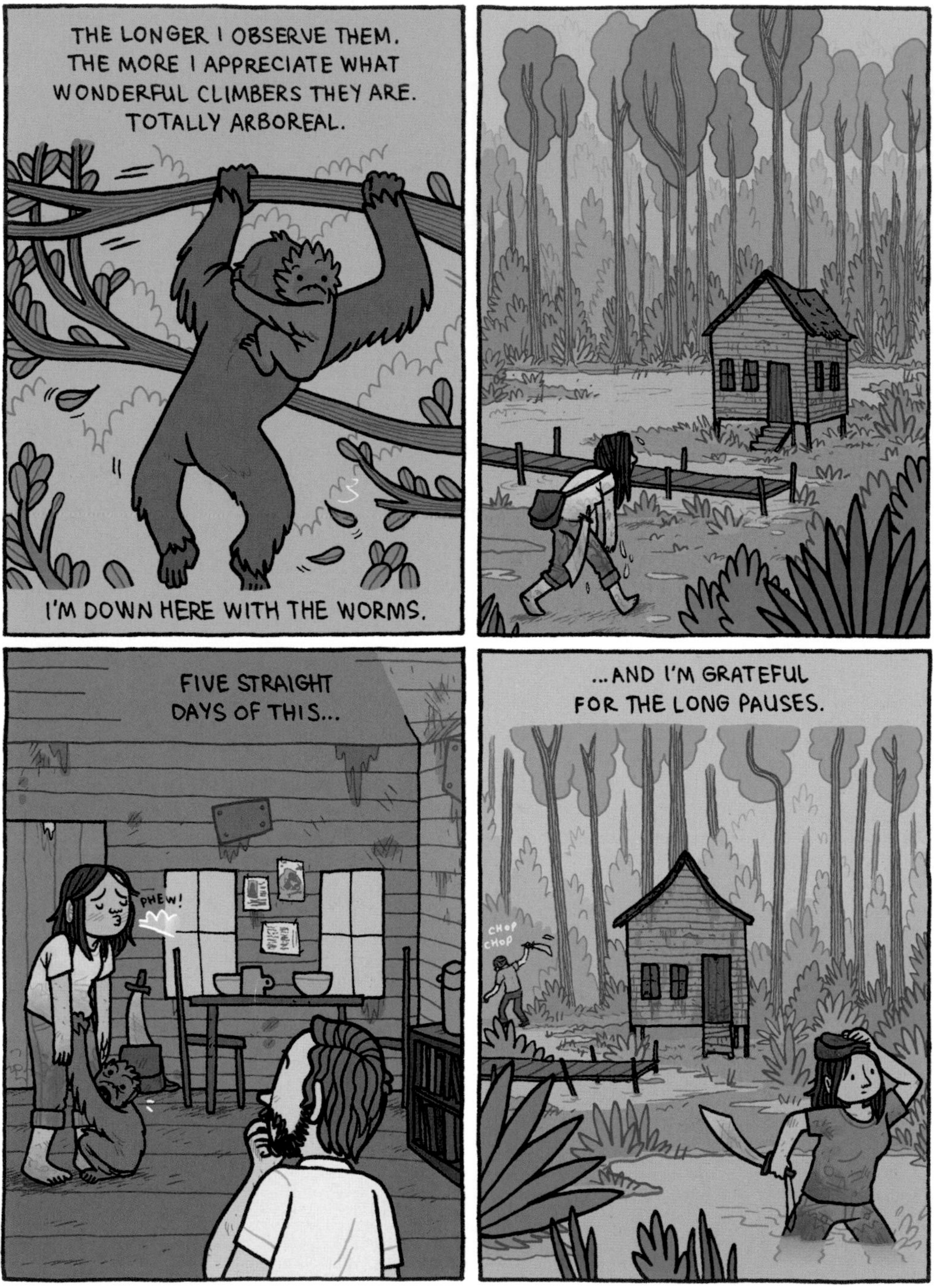
THE LONGER I OBSERVE THEM.
THE MORE I APPRECIATE WHAT WONDERFUL CLIMBERS THEY ARE. TOTALLY ARBOREAL.
I'M DOWN HERE WITH THE WORMS.
FIVE STRAIGHT DAYS OF THIS...
PHEW!
...AND I'M GRATEFUL FOR THE LONG PAUSES.
CHOP CHOP

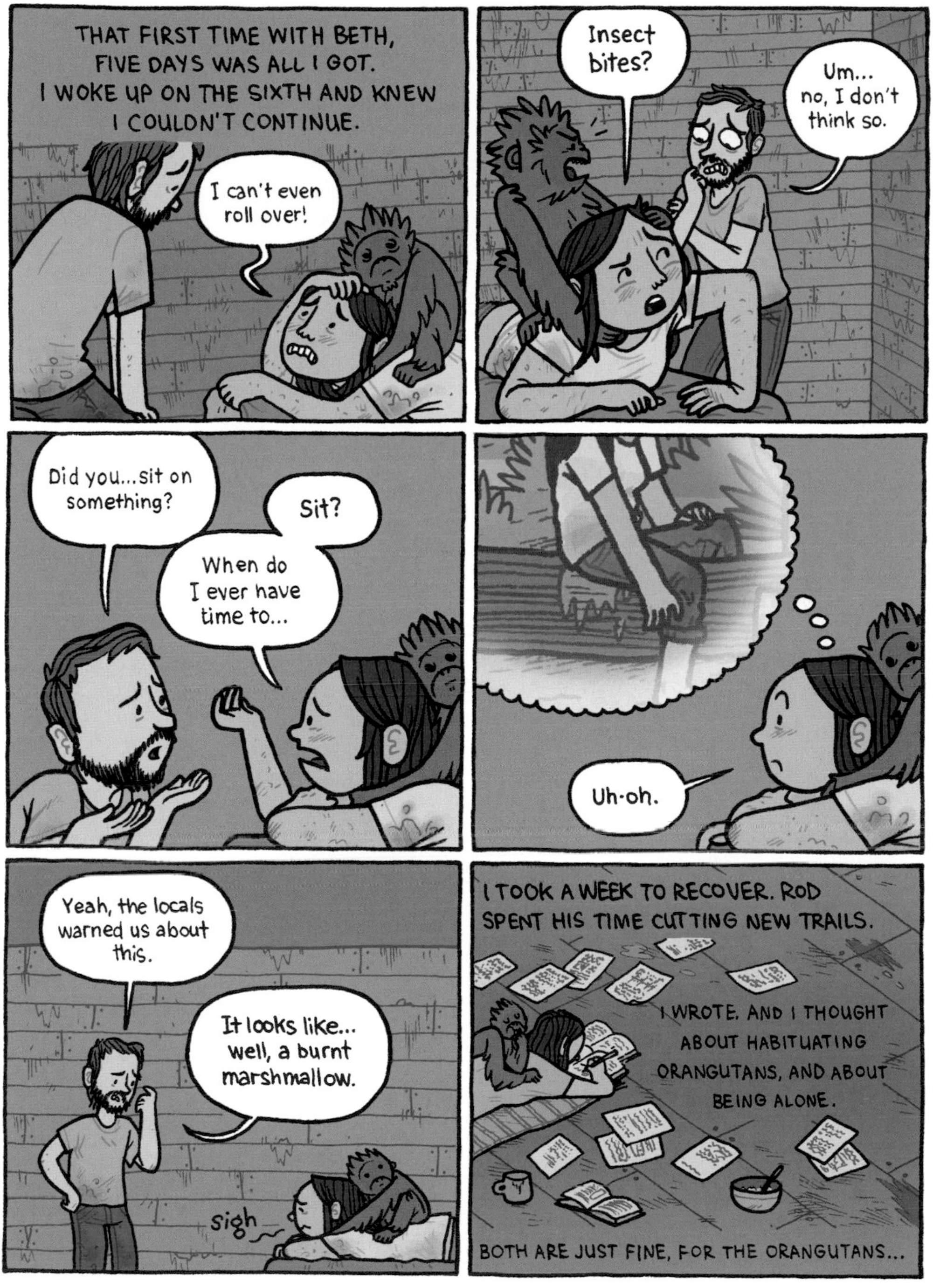
THAT FIRST TIME WITH BETH, FIVE DAYS WAS ALL I GOT. I WOKE UP ON THE SIXTH AND KNEW I COULDN'T CONTINUE.
I can't even roll over!
Insect bites?
Um... no, I don't think so.
Did you...sit on something?
Sit?
When do I ever have time to...
Uh-oh.
Yeah, the locals warned us about this.
It looks like... well, a burnt marshmallow.
sigh
I TOOK A WEEK TO RECOVER. ROD SPENT HIS TIME CUTTING NEW TRAILS.
I WROTE, AND I THOUGHT ABOUT HABITUATING ORANGUTANS, AND ABOUT BEING ALONE.
BOTH ARE JUST FINE, FOR THE ORANGUTANS...

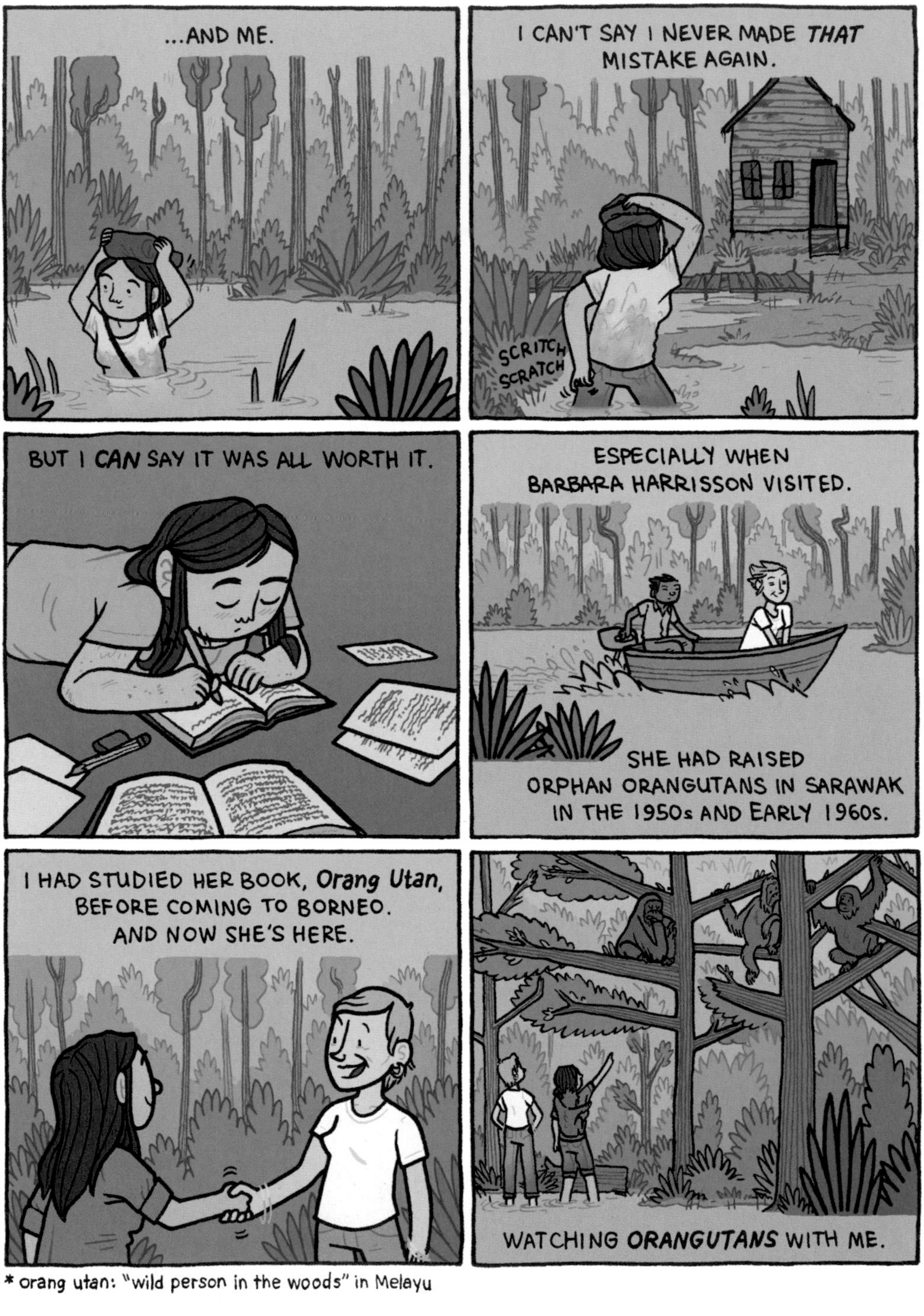
...AND ME.
I CAN'T SAY I NEVER MADE THAT MISTAKE AGAIN.
SCRITCH SCRATCH
BUT I CAN SAY IT WAS ALL WORTH IT.
ESPECIALLY WHEN BARBARA HARRISSON VISITED.
SHE HAD RAISED ORPHAN ORANGUTANS IN SARAWAK IN THE 1950s AND EARLY 1960s.
I HAD STUDIED HER BOOK, Orang Utan, BEFORE COMING TO BORNEO. AND NOW SHE'S HERE.
WATCHING ORANGUTANS WITH ME.

* orang utan: "wild person in the woods" in Melayu

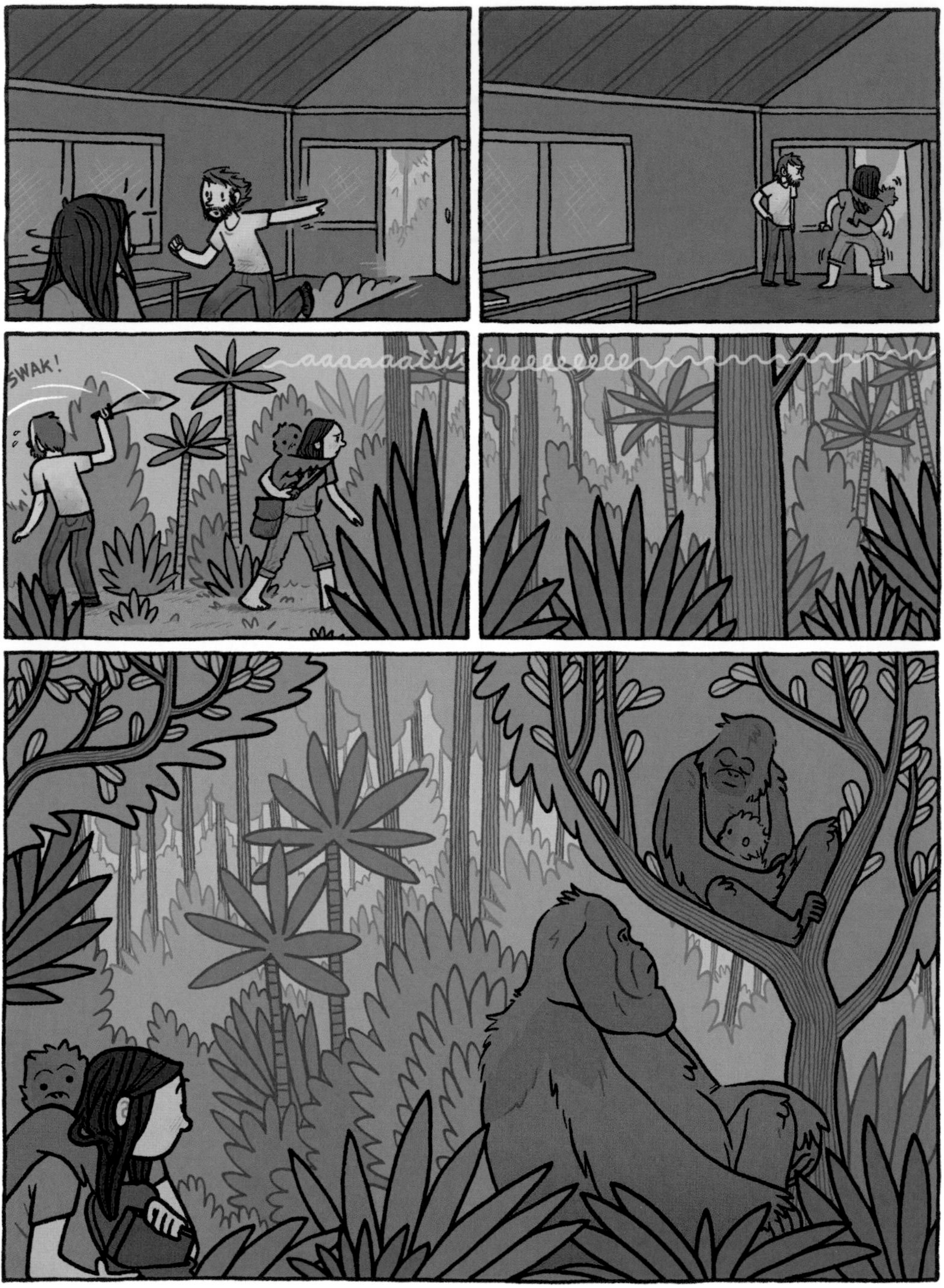
SWAK!

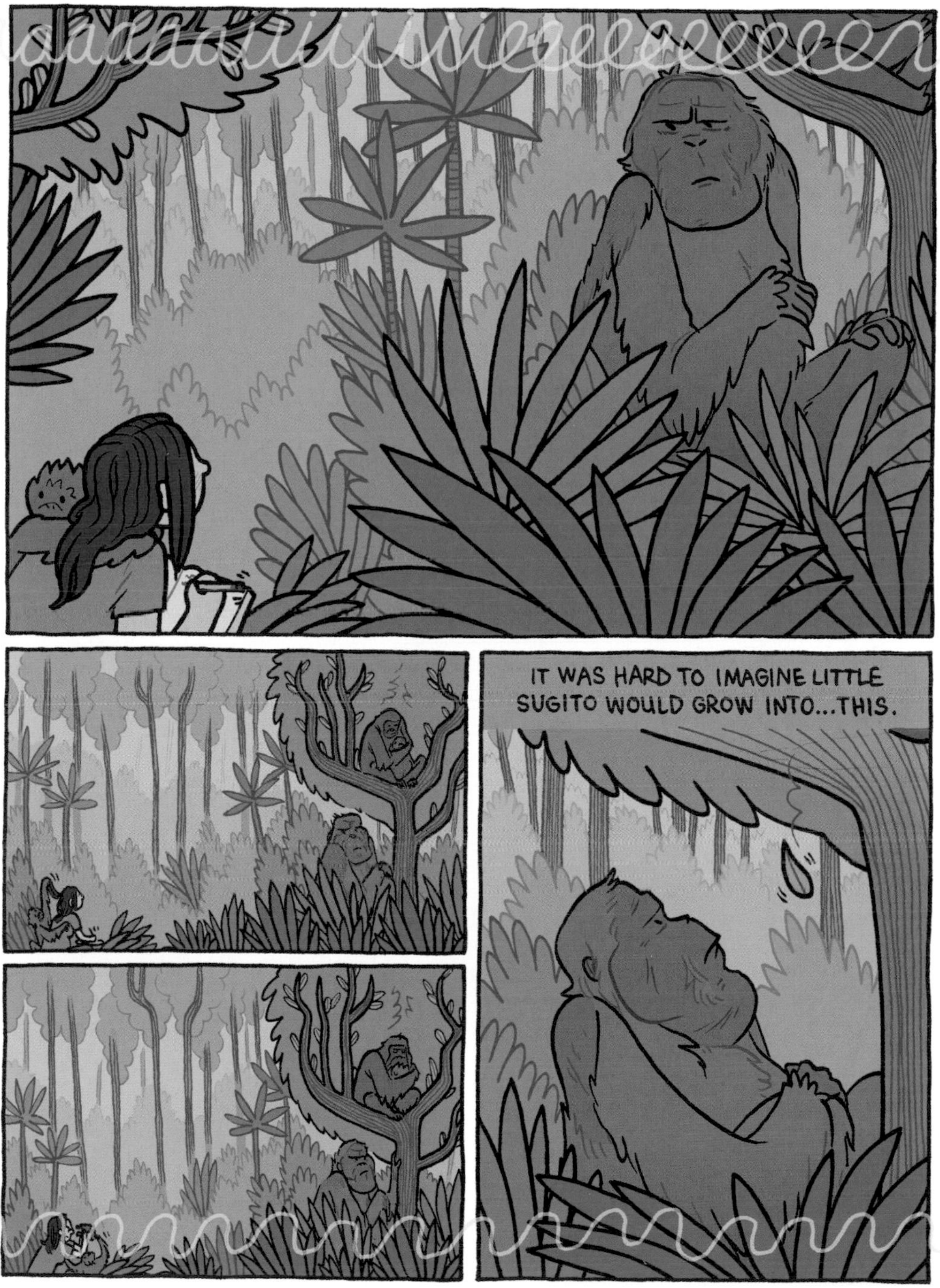
IT WAS HARD TO IMAGINE LITTLE SUGITO WOULD GROW INTO...THIS.

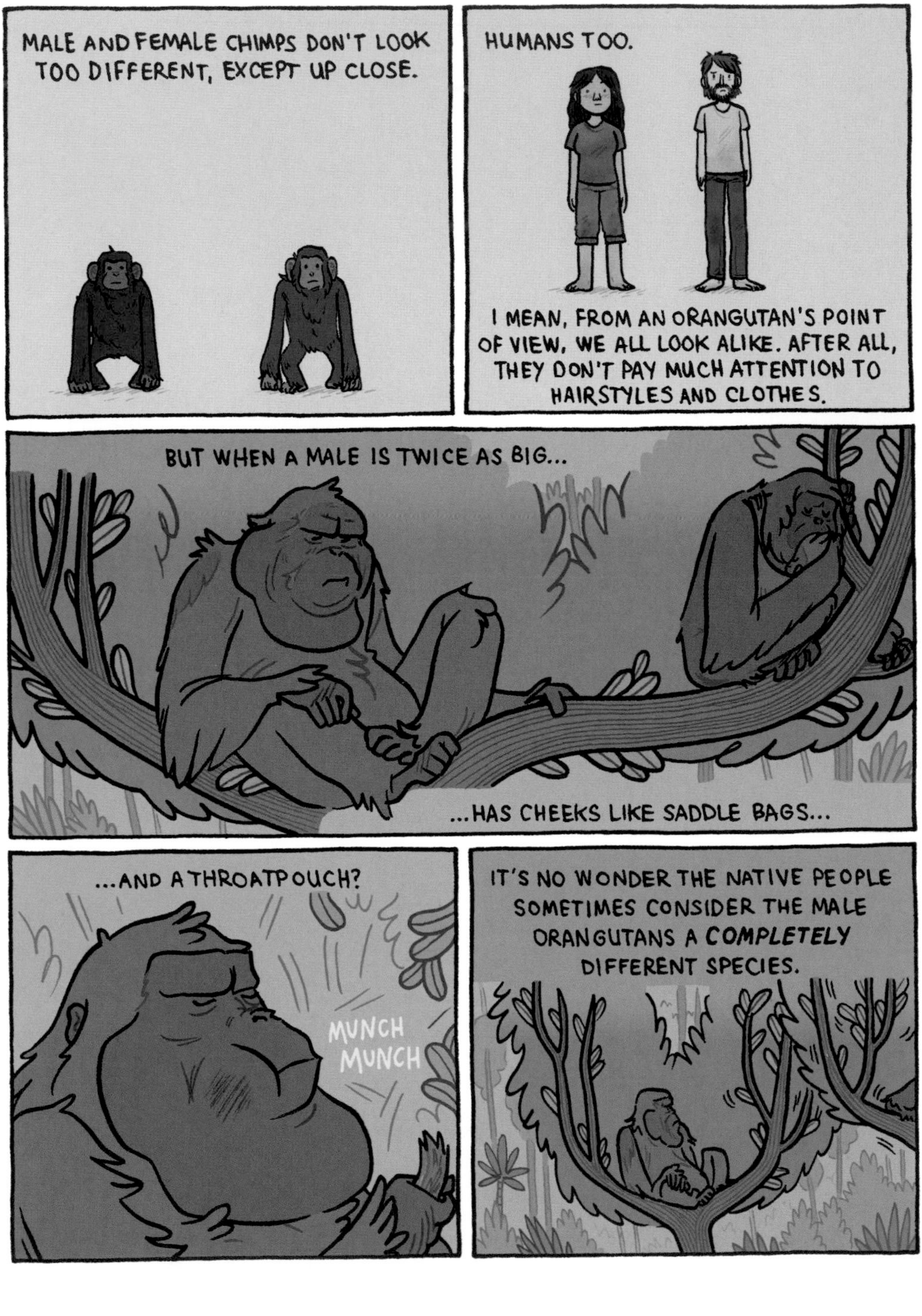
MALE AND FEMALE CHIMPS DON'T LOOK TOO DIFFERENT, EXCEPT UP CLOSE.
HUMANS TOO.
I MEAN, FROM AN ORANGUTAN'S POINT OF VIEW, WE ALL LOOK ALIKE. AFTER ALL, THEY DON'T PAY MUCH ATTENTION TO HAIRSTYLES AND CLOTHES.
BUT WHEN A MALE IS TWICE AS BIG...
...HAS CHEEKS LIKE SADDLE BAGS...
...AND A THROAT POUCH?
MUNCH MUNCH
IT'S NO WONDER THE NATIVE PEOPLE SOMETIMES CONSIDER THE MALE ORANGUTANS A COMPLETELY DIFFERENT SPECIES.

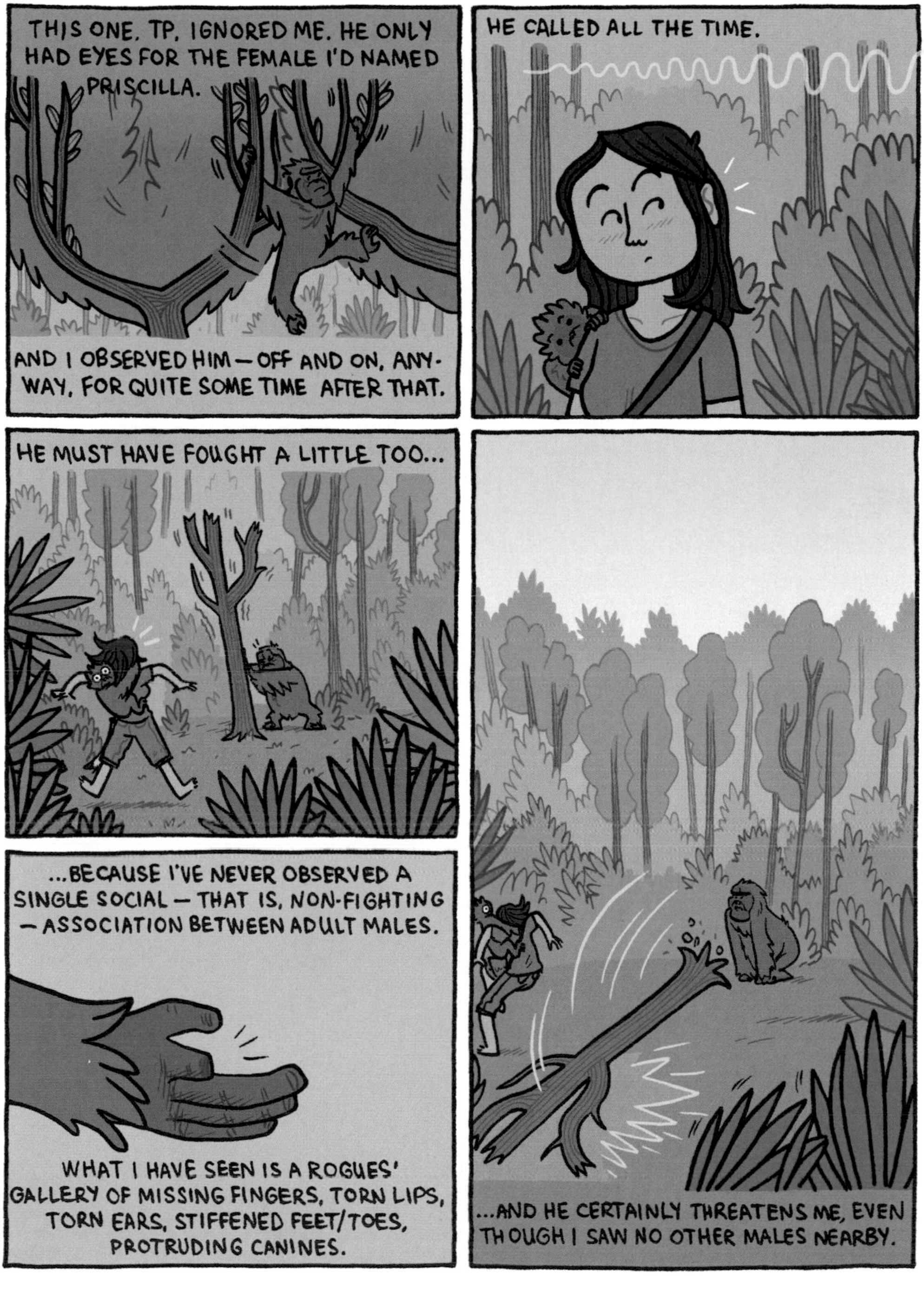
THIS ONE, TP, IGNORED ME. HE ONLY HAD EYES FOR THE FEMALE I'D NAMED PRISCILLA.
AND I OBSERVED HIM — OFF AND ON, ANYWAY, FOR QUITE SOME TIME AFTER THAT.
HE CALLED ALL THE TIME.
HE MUST HAVE FOUGHT A LITTLE TOO...
...AND HE CERTAINLY THREATENS ME, EVEN THOUGH I SAW NO OTHER MALES NEARBY.
...BECAUSE I'VE NEVER OBSERVED A SINGLE SOCIAL — THAT IS, NON-FIGHTING — ASSOCIATION BETWEEN ADULT MALES.
WHAT I HAVE SEEN IS A ROGUES' GALLERY OF MISSING FINGERS, TORN LIPS, TORN EARS, STIFFENED FEET/TOES, PROTRUDING CANINES.

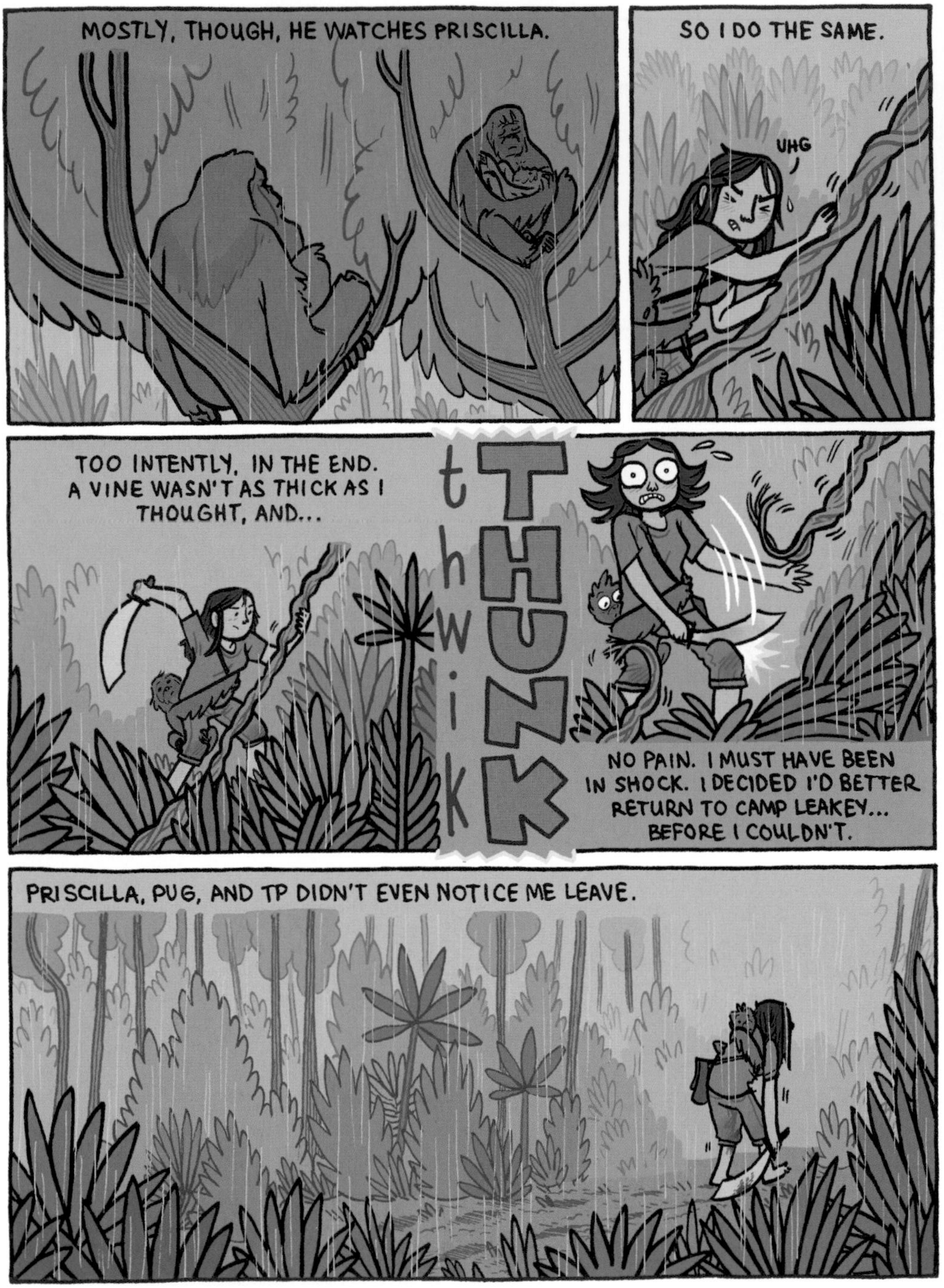
MOSTLY, THOUGH, HE WATCHES PRISCILLA.
SO I DO THE SAME.
UHG
TOO INTENTLY, IN THE END. A VINE WASN'T AS THICK AS I THOUGHT, AND...
thwik
THUNK
NO PAIN. I MUST HAVE BEEN IN SHOCK. I DECIDED I'D BETTER RETURN TO CAMP LEAKEY... BEFORE I COULDN'T.
PRISCILLA, PUG, AND TP DIDN'T EVEN NOTICE ME LEAVE.

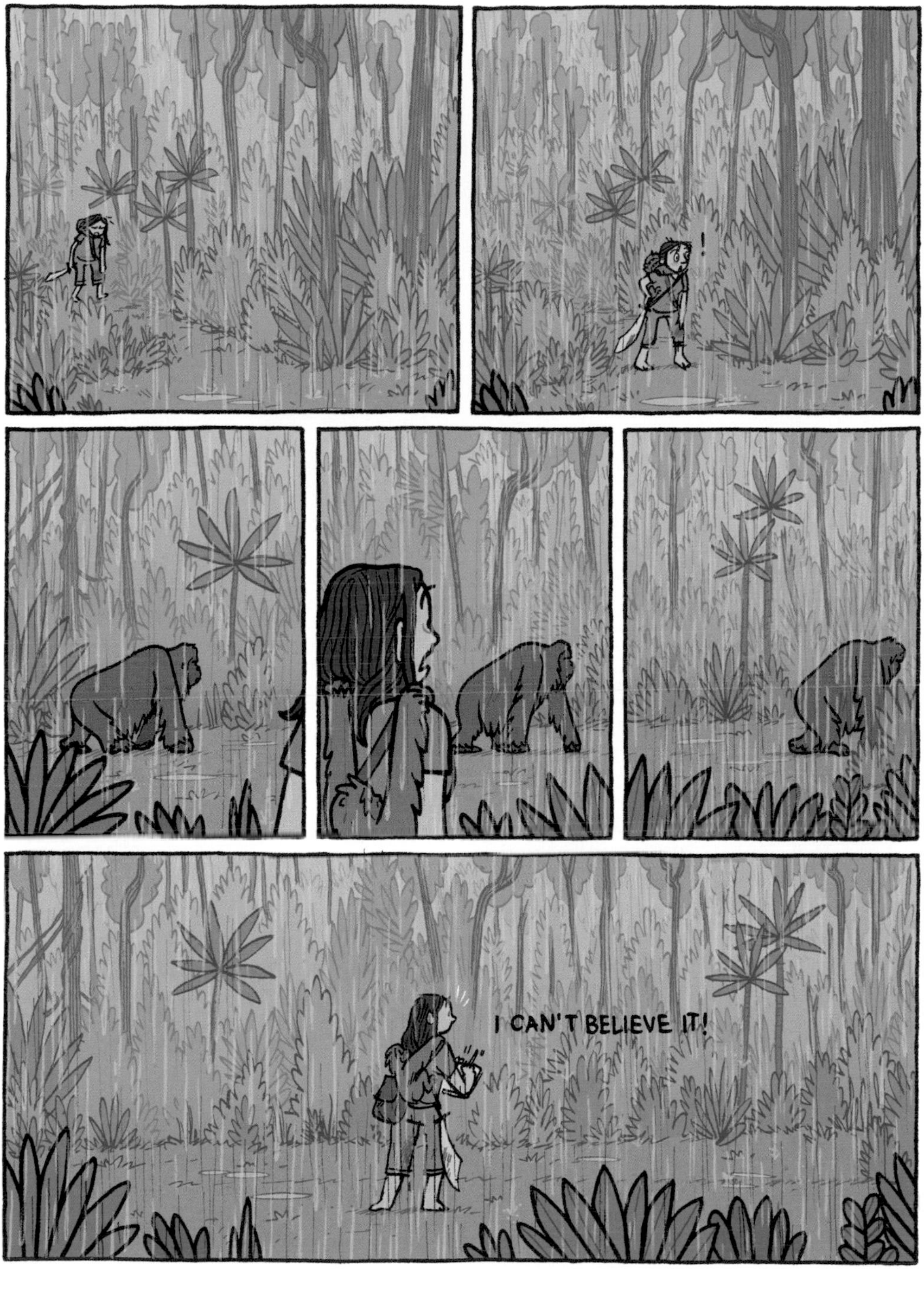
I CAN'T BELIEVE IT!

115

Part 4: The **Trimates**

117

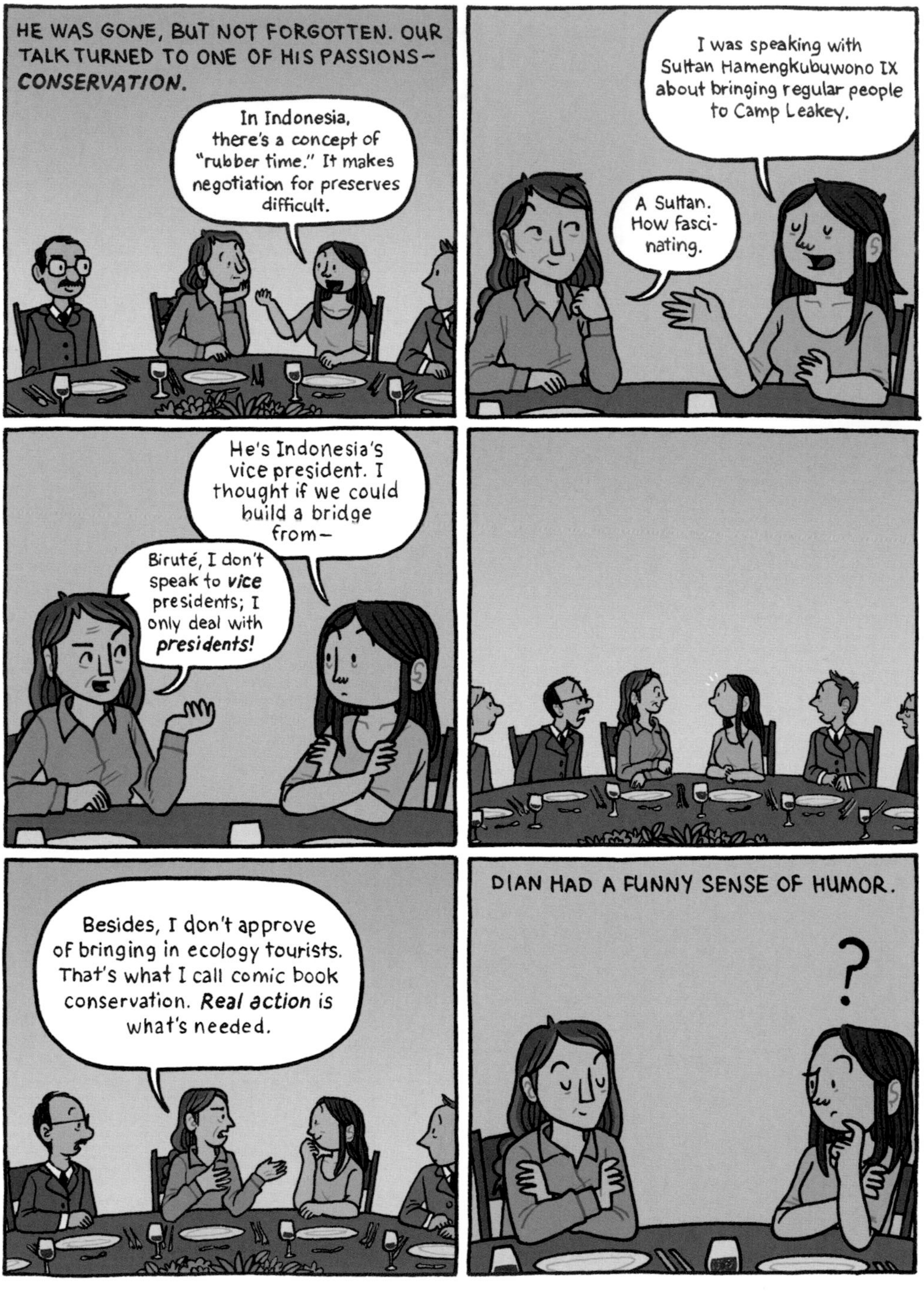
HE WAS GONE, BUT NOT FORGOTTEN. OUR TALK TURNED TO ONE OF HIS PASSIONS— CONSERVATION.
In Indonesia, there's a concept of "rubber time." It makes negotiation for preserves difficult.
I was speaking with Sultan Hamengkubuwono IX about bringing regular people to Camp Leakey.
A Sultan. How fascinating.
He's Indonesia's vice president. I thought if we could build a bridge from—
Biruté, I don't speak to vice presidents; I only deal with presidents!
Besides, I don't approve of bringing in ecology tourists. That's what I call comic book conservation. Real action is what's needed.
DIAN HAD A FUNNY SENSE OF HUMOR.
?

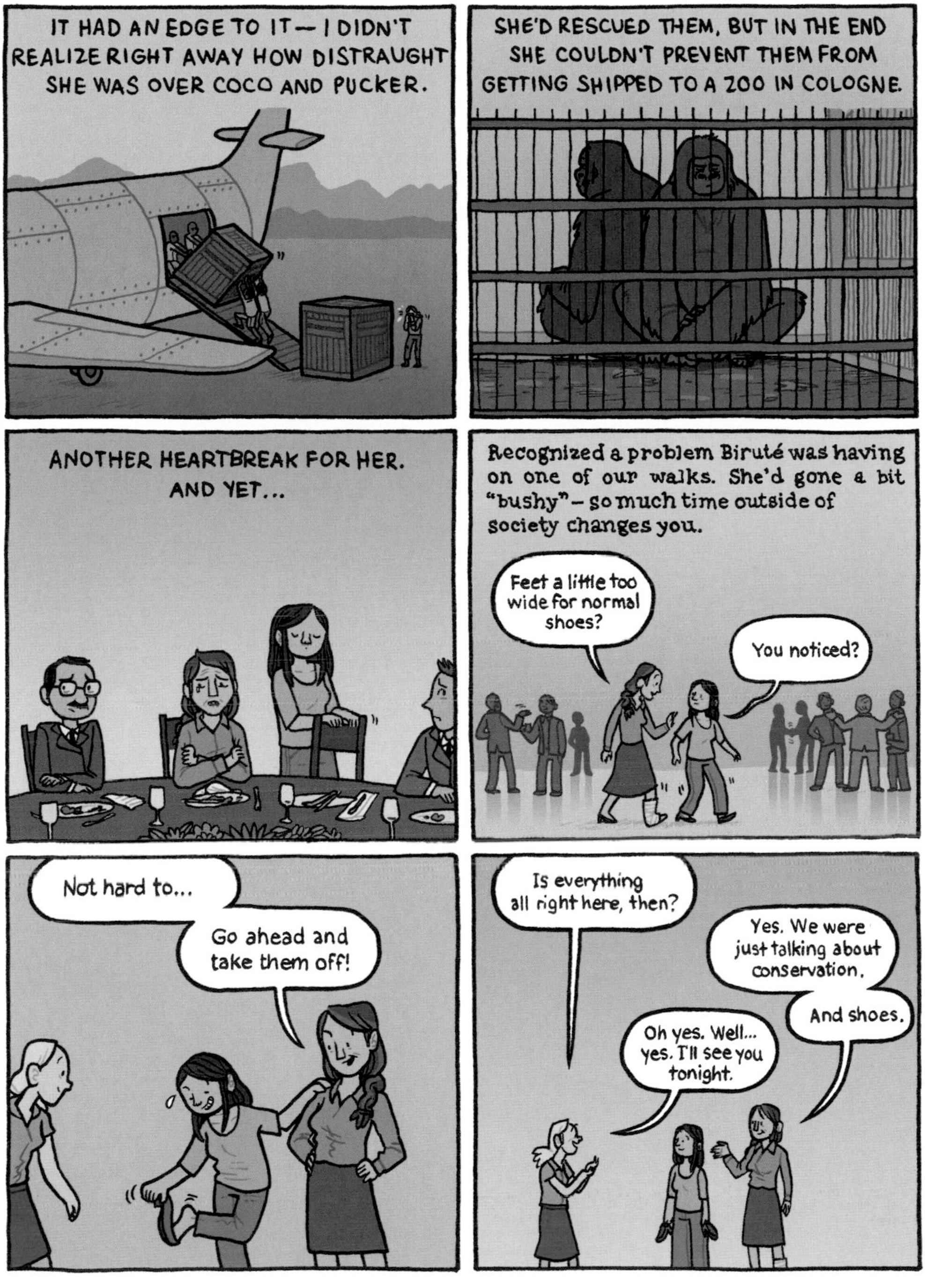
IT HAD AN EDGE TO IT — I DIDN'T REALIZE RIGHT AWAY HOW DISTRAUGHT SHE WAS OVER COCO AND PUCKER.
SHE'D RESCUED THEM, BUT IN THE END SHE COULDN'T PREVENT THEM FROM GETTING SHIPPED TO A ZOO IN COLOGNE.
ANOTHER HEARTBREAK FOR HER. AND YET...
Recognized a problem Biruté was having on one of our walks. She'd gone a bit "bushy" – so much time outside of society changes you.
Feet a little too wide for normal shoes?
You noticed?
Not hard to...
Go ahead and take them off!
Is everything all right here, then?
Yes. We were just talking about conservation.
And shoes.
Oh yes. Well... yes. I'll see you tonight.

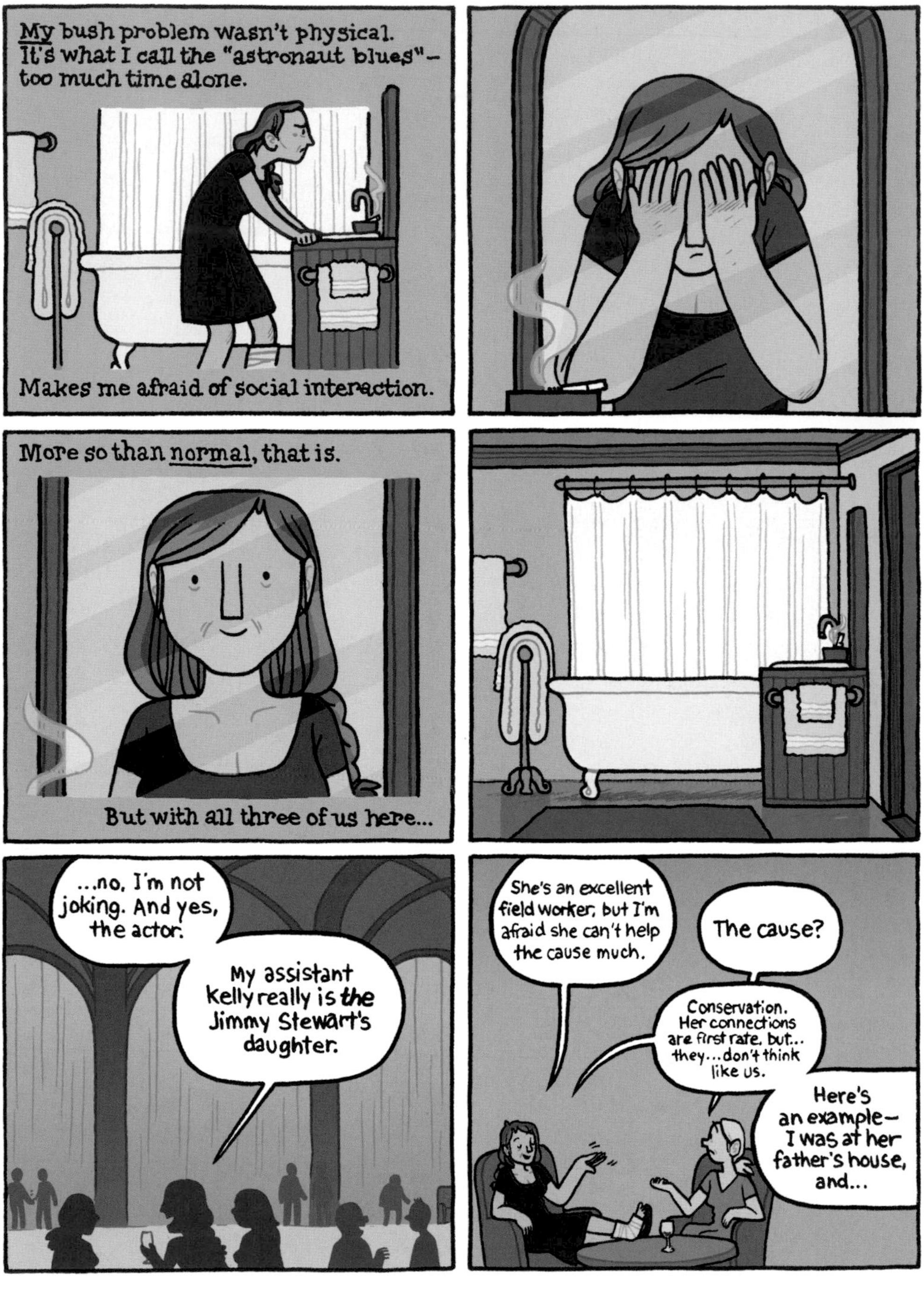
My bush problem wasn't physical. It's what I call the "astronaut blues"—too much time alone.
Makes me afraid of social interaction.
More so than normal, that is.
But with all three of us here...
...no, I'm not joking. And yes, the actor.
My assistant Kelly really is the Jimmy Stewart's daughter.
She's an excellent field worker, but I'm afraid she can't help the cause much.
The cause?
Conservation. Her connections are first rate, but... they...don't think like us.
Here's an example—I was at her father's house, and...

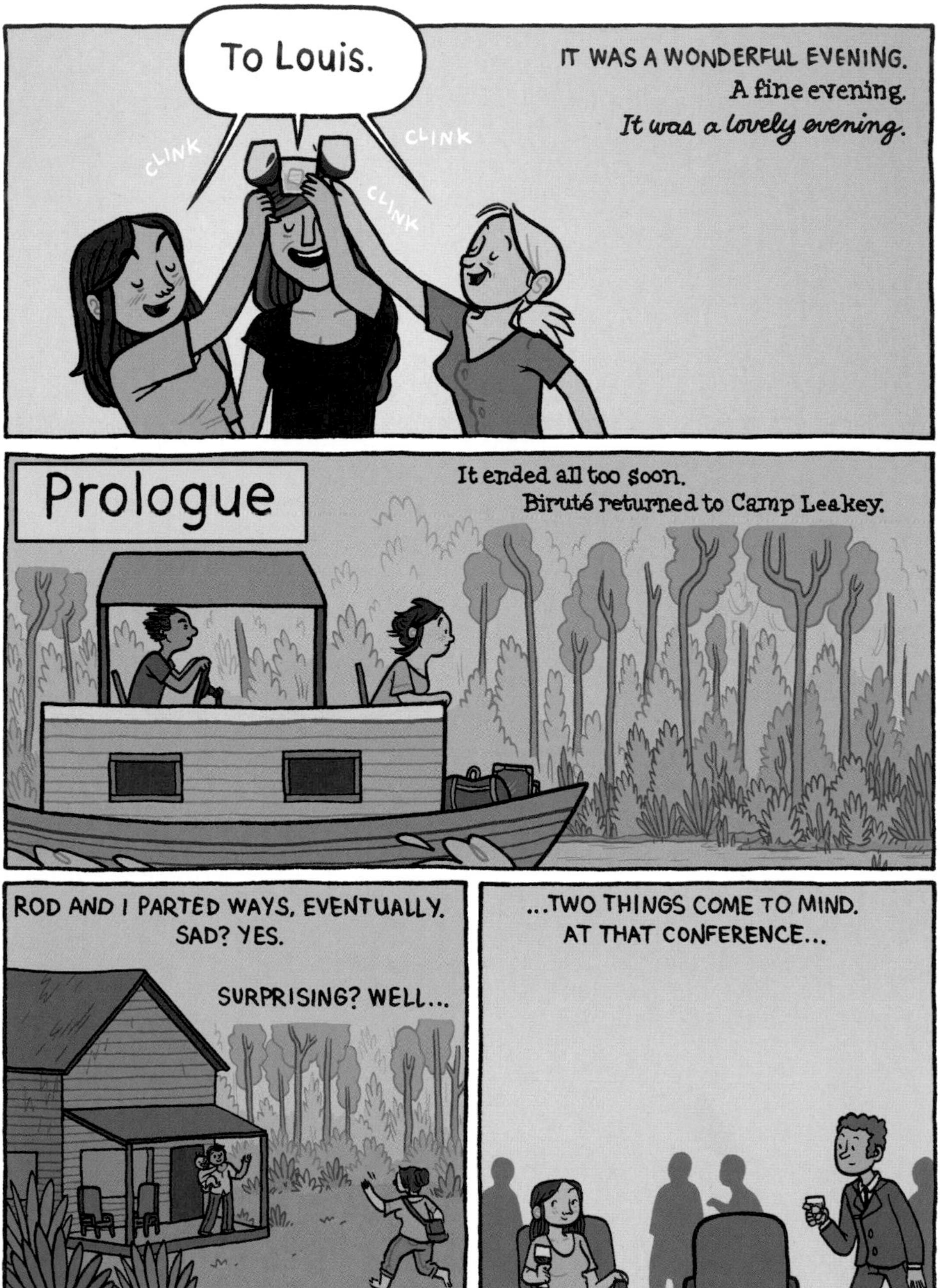
To Louis.
CLINK
CLINK
CLINK
IT WAS A WONDERFUL EVENING.
A fine evening.
It was a lovely evening.
Prologue
It ended all too soon.
Biruté returned to Camp Leakey.
ROD AND I PARTED WAYS, EVENTUALLY.
SAD? YES.
SURPRISING? WELL...
...TWO THINGS COME TO MIND.
AT THAT CONFERENCE...

123

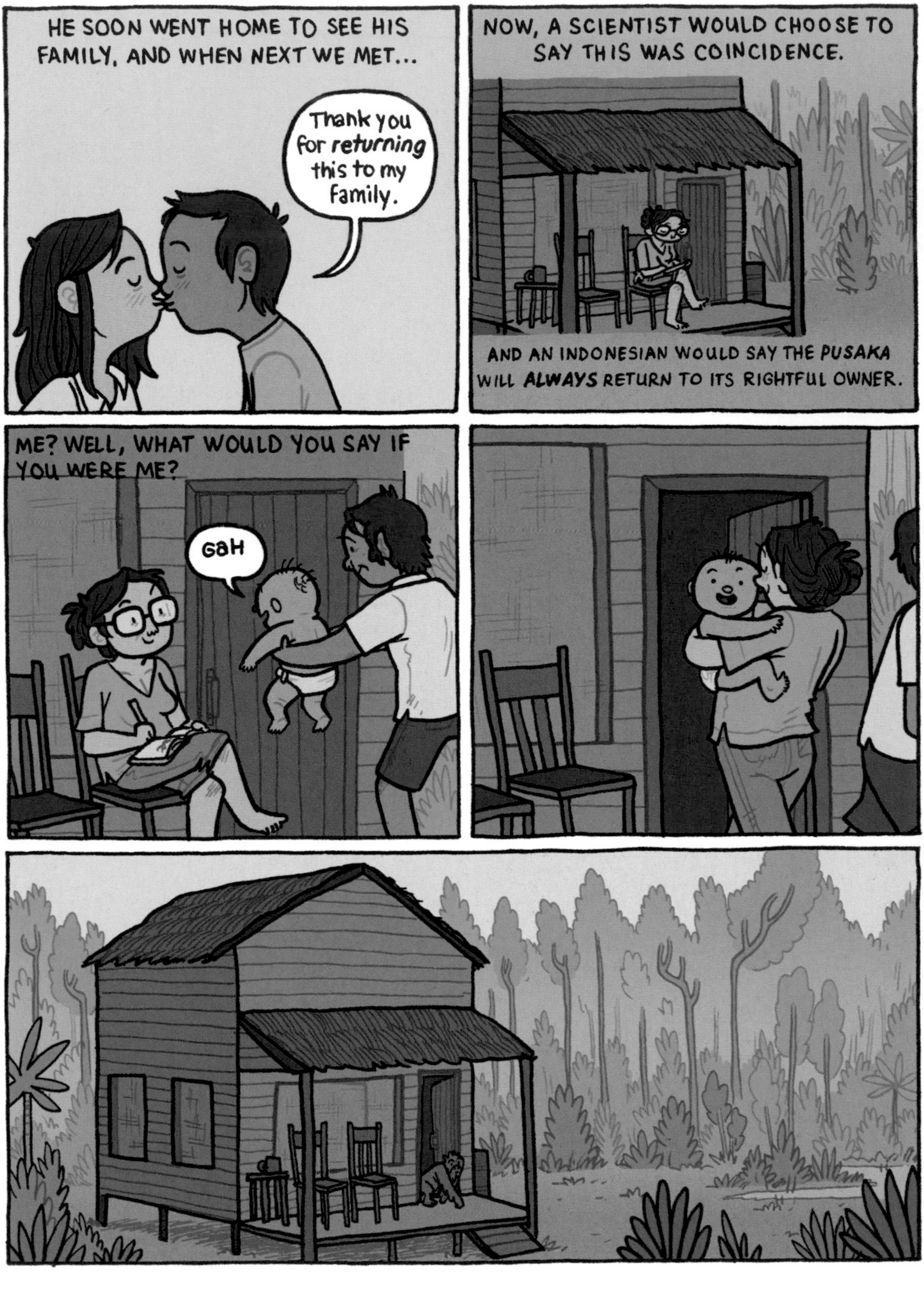
HE SOON WENT HOME TO SEE HIS FAMILY, AND WHEN NEXT WE MET...
Thank you for *returning* this to my family.
NOW, A SCIENTIST WOULD CHOOSE TO SAY THIS WAS COINCIDENCE.
AND AN INDONESIAN WOULD SAY THE *PUSAKA* WILL ***ALWAYS*** RETURN TO ITS RIGHTFUL OWNER.
ME? WELL, WHAT WOULD YOU SAY IF YOU WERE ME?
GAH

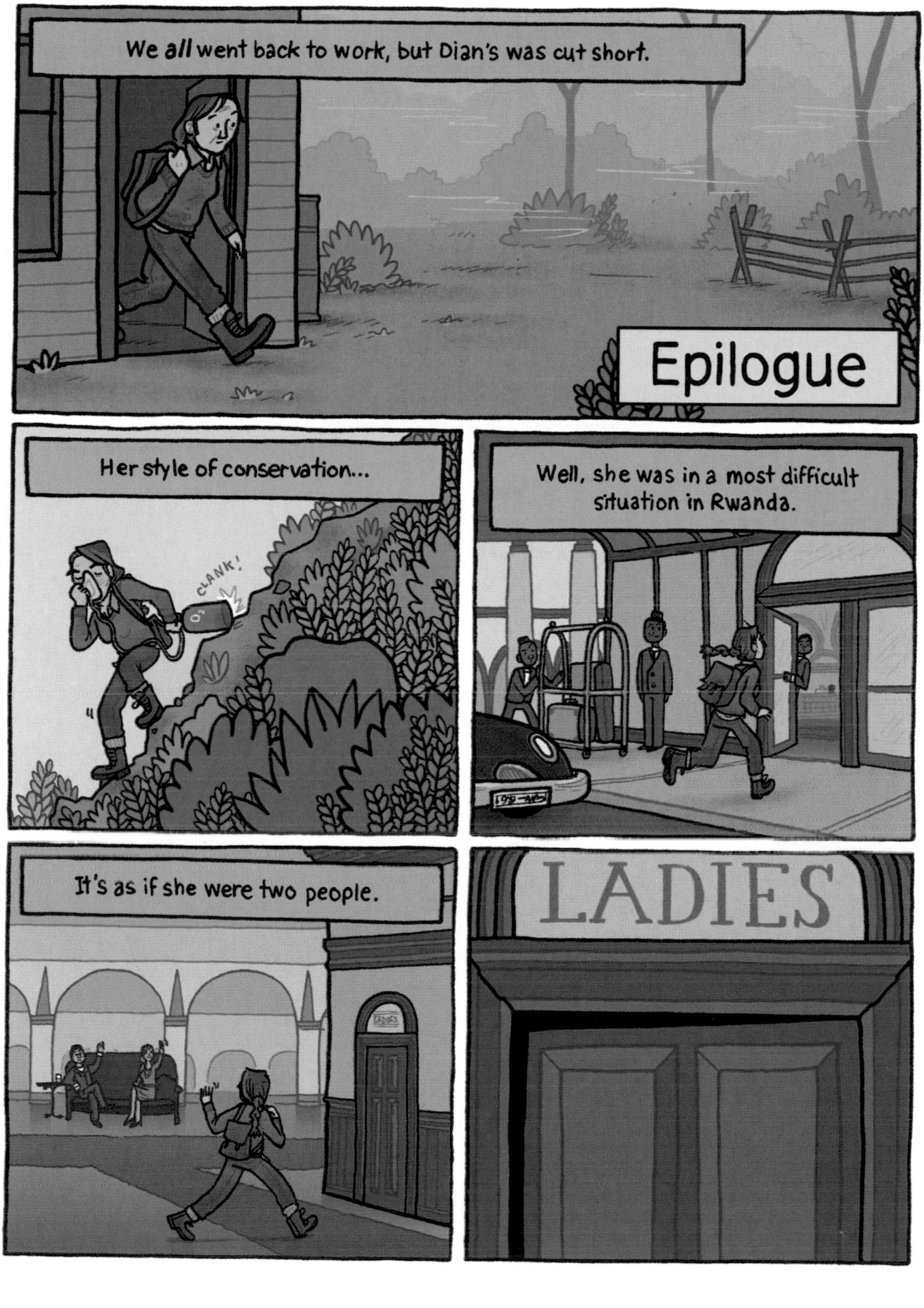
We all went back to work, but Dian's was cut short.
Epilogue
Her style of conservation...
CLANK!
O_2
Well, she was in a most difficult situation in Rwanda.
It's as if she were two people.
LADIES
LADIES

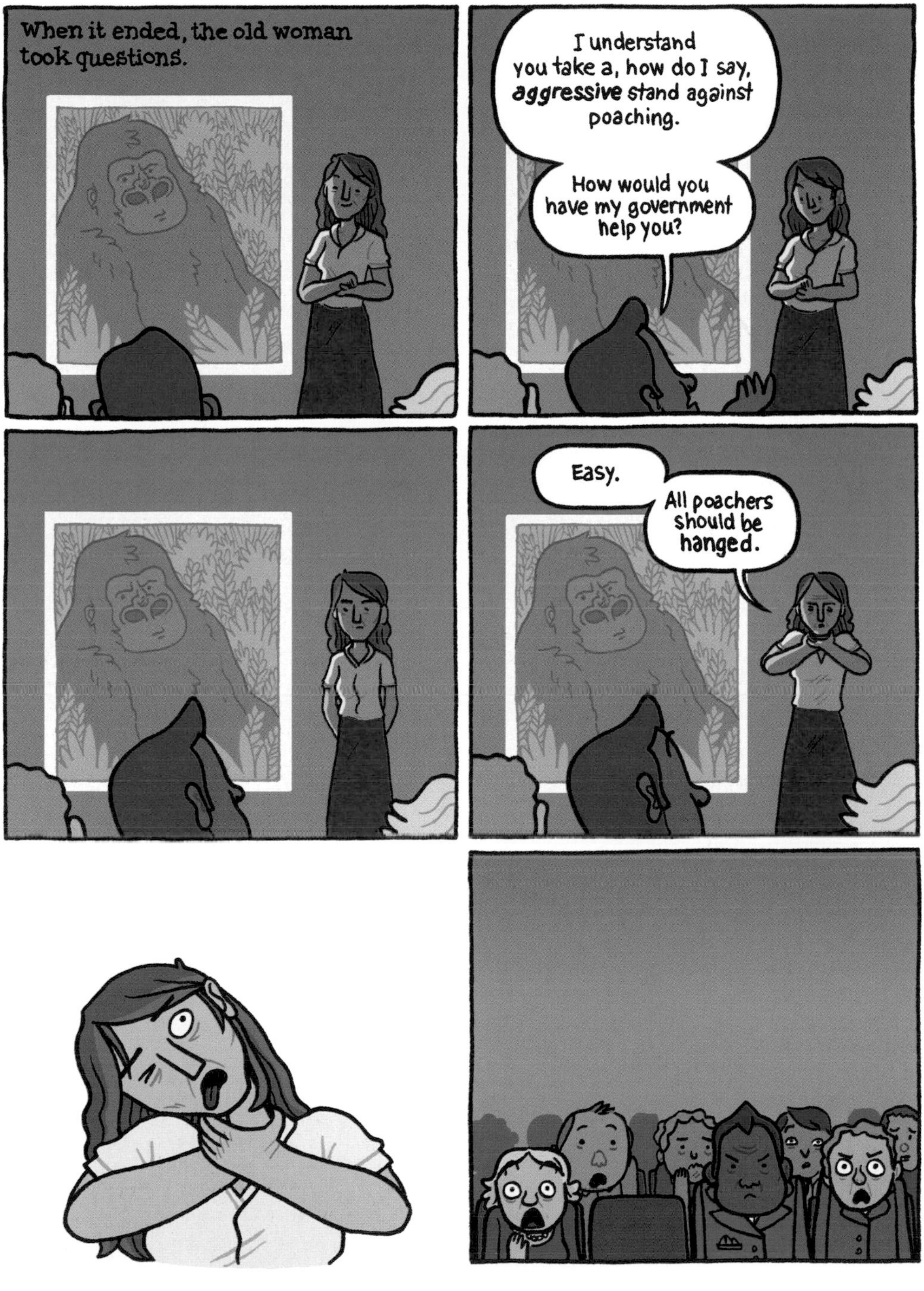
When it ended, the old woman took questions.
I understand you take a, how do I say, aggressive stand against poaching.
How would you have my government help you?
Easy.
All poachers should be hanged.

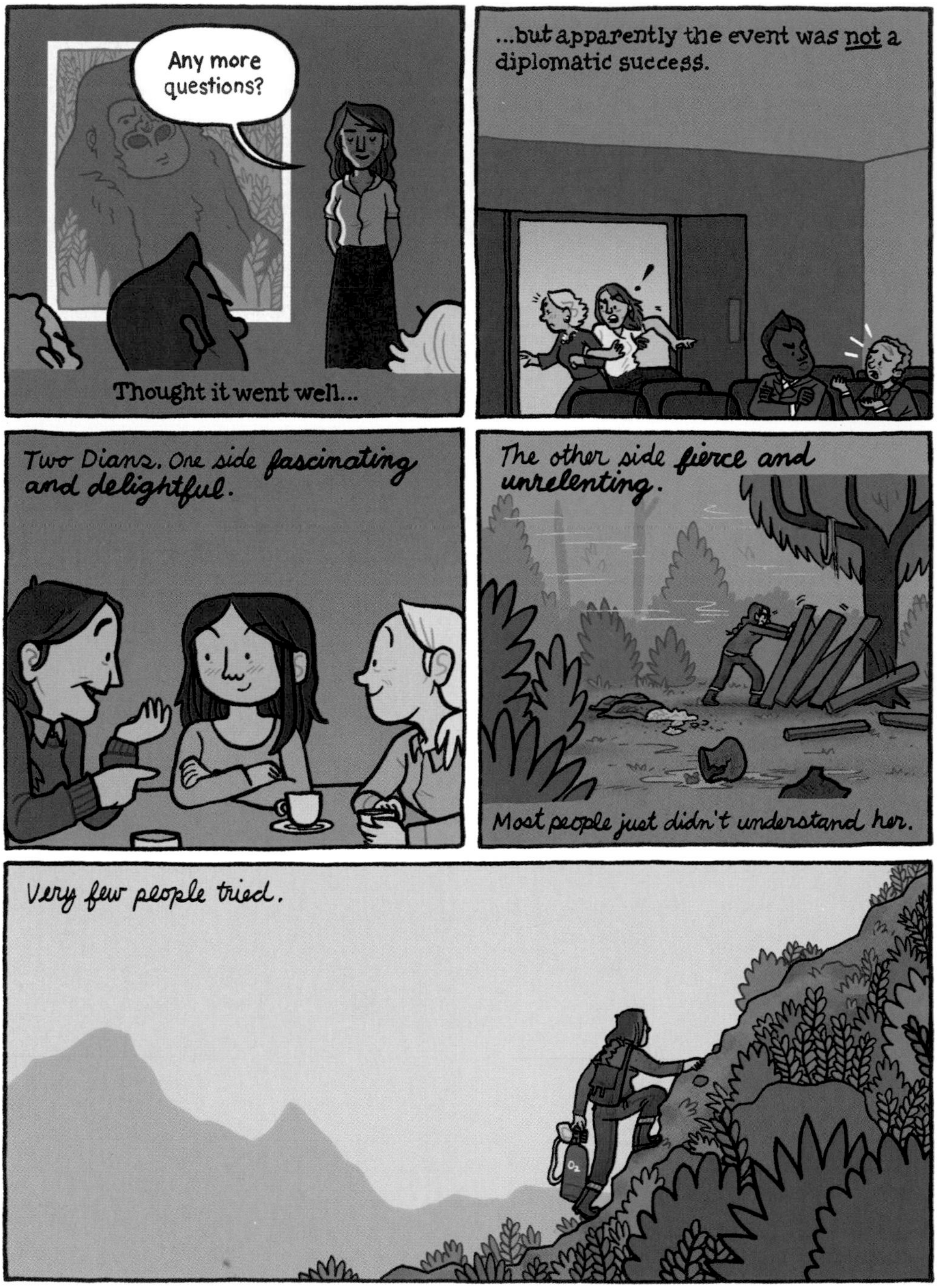

Any more questions?
Thought it went well...
...but apparently the event was not a diplomatic success.
Two Dians. One side fascinating and delightful.
The other side fierce and unrelenting.
Most people just didn't understand her.
Very few people tried.

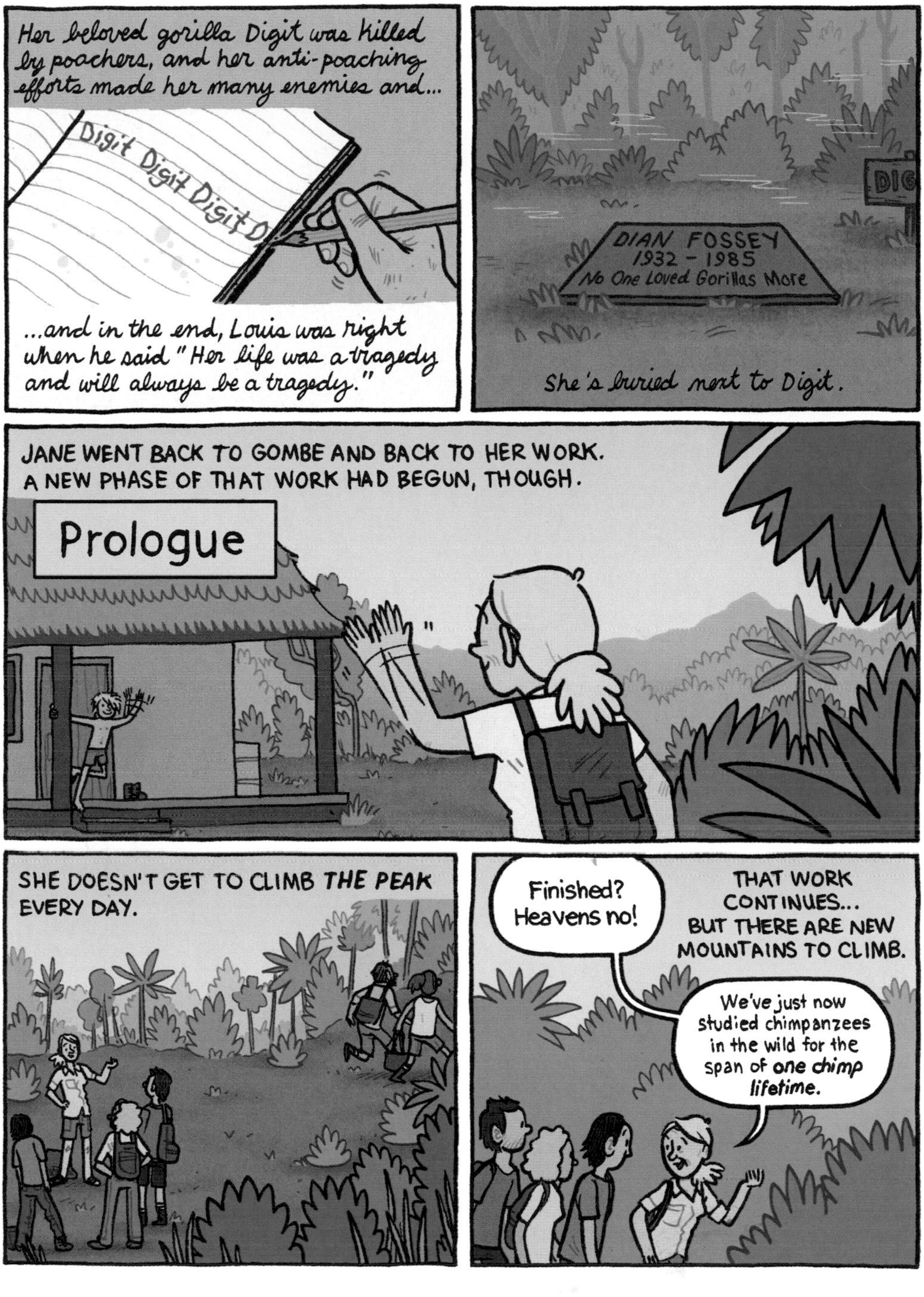
Her beloved gorilla Digit was killed by poachers, and her anti-poaching efforts made her many enemies and...
Digit Digit Digit Digit D
...and in the end, Louis was right when he said "Her life was a tragedy and will always be a tragedy."
DIG
DIAN FOSSEY
1932 - 1985
No One Loved Gorillas More
She's buried next to Digit.
JANE WENT BACK TO GOMBE AND BACK TO HER WORK.
A NEW PHASE OF THAT WORK HAD BEGUN, THOUGH.
Prologue
SHE DOESN'T GET TO CLIMB THE PEAK EVERY DAY.
Finished? Heavens no!
THAT WORK CONTINUES... BUT THERE ARE NEW MOUNTAINS TO CLIMB.
We've just now studied chimpanzees in the wild for the span of one chimp lifetime.

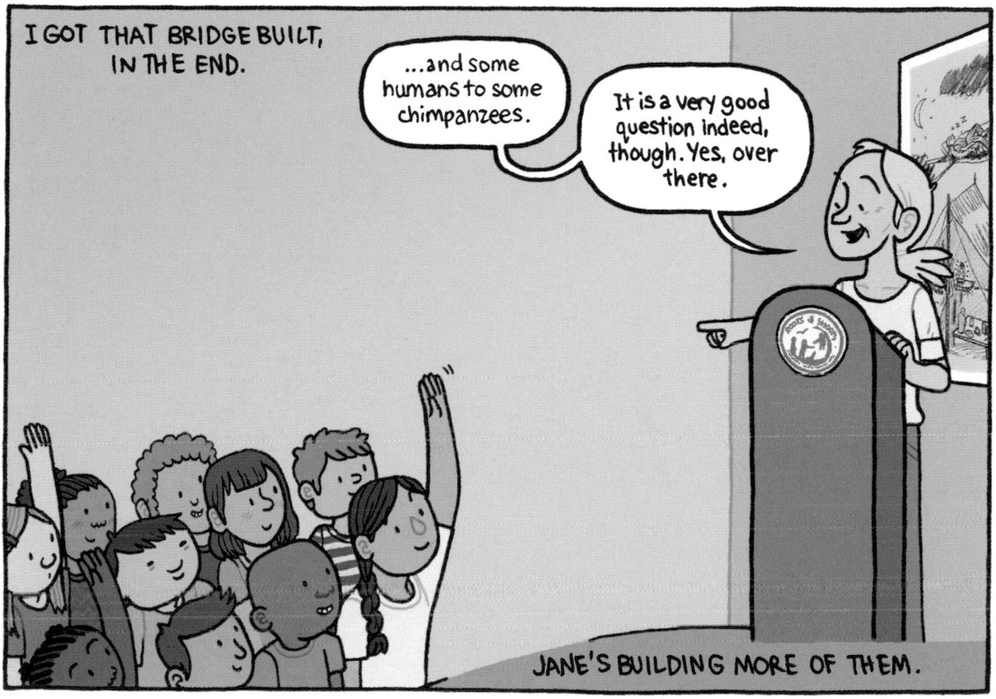
I GOT THAT BRIDGE BUILT, IN THE END.
...and some humans to some chimpanzees.
It is a very good question indeed, though. Yes, over there.
JANE'S BUILDING MORE OF THEM.

AFTERWORD

Maris and I didn't get up before dawn in the jungle, we didn't climb mountains, and we didn't wade through swamps either. So we didn't observe Jane Goodall, Dian Fossey, and Biruté Galdikas the same way they observed chimpanzees, gorillas, and orangutans.

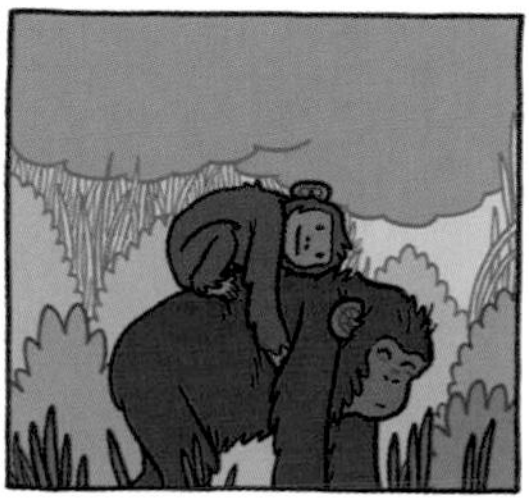

As a result, some of what you just read is fiction. You probably guessed that already, but some of it would have been fiction even if we had done all the things our heroes did. The reason is, real lives don't behave like stories, complete with tidy beginnings, middles, and ends. (Science doesn't even have an end!) And some of what I write now, late at night here in Michigan with the only animal of any size nearby being my cat, is probably fiction too, since I'm writing this long after finishing the script and sending it to Maris. Memories fade, and writing a story isn't science, so I didn't keep a lab notebook to remind myself of the failures, false starts, and occasional a-ha! moments that went into putting this book together.

So, can you trust what I wrote, or what Maris drew? Well, yes . . . mostly.

Here's what I mean: We did study their lives, read a lot about primates, and try to get all the significant details right. That's not to say that every single detail isn't important in science, but we wanted to tell a story and not make a textbook. So we had to pick and choose whether and when to leave something out, or compress a week's (or a month's, or a year's) worth of their hard work down to something you could read in much less than a week or a month or a year. To do

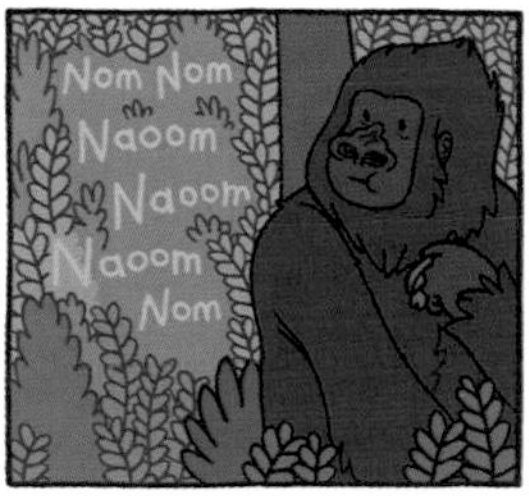
Nom Nom
Naoom
Naoom
Naoom
Nom

this I put together detailed timelines and looked for parts where events, discoveries—and just as important—themes and ideas complemented each other. Maris studied primate behavior, anatomy, and their environments. And we both listened to the sounds the animals make and studied the things the scientists

said and did, in their own words whenever possible, and asked ourselves and each other lots of questions about how to weave three remarkable lives into one story.

What kind of person does it take to do this kind of work? How hard is it?

When did our understanding of what it means to be a primate begin? And why is it important? Those are the questions we hope you had when you started the book, and hope you've gotten some answers by the end.* But by now you've guessed, and guessed right, that the end of this book isn't the end of the story.

There's a lot more you can learn about Jane Goodall, Dian Fossey, and Biruté Galdikas, and we recommend starting with the list below. It includes books we consulted all the time when we made this one, and we know you'll enjoy reading more about these three amazing women.

* My answers to the first three questions are: Smart and tough. Very. Not as long ago as you might think and we're not done yet. As for why this is important . . . visit www.gt-labs.com/blog/2013/05/primates.html and leave a comment. We want to hear what you think!

BIBLIOGRAPHY

JANE GOODALL: TRAILBLAZER
   In the Shadow of Man (NY: Mariner Books, 2000).
   Through a Window (NY: Mariner Books, 2000).
   Africa in My Blood: An Autobiography in Letters: The Early Years
      (NY: Mariner Books, 2001).
   Beyond Innocence: An Autobiography in Letters: The Later Years
      (NY: Mariner Books, 2001).
   Jane Goodall: The Woman Who Redefined Man, by Dale Peterson
      (NY: Houghton Mifflin, 2006).

DIAN FOSSEY: CONSERVATOR
   Gorillas in the Mist (NY: Mariner Books, 2000).
   Woman in the Mists, by Farley Mowat (NY: Warner Books, 1988).
   No One Loved Gorillas More: Dian Fossey, Letters from the Mist, by Camilla
      de la Bédoyère with photographs by Bob Campbell (Washington, DC:
      National Geographic, 2005).

BIRUTÉ GALDIKAS: AMBASSADOR
   Reflections of Eden (Boston: Little, Brown, 1995).
   Orangutan Odyssey, with Nancy Briggs, photographs by Karl Ammann
      (NY: Harry N. Abrams, 1999).
   Great Ape Odyssey, photographs by Karl Ammann (NY: Harry N. Abrams,
      2005).

Other good books to read include

Ancestral Passions: The Leakey Family and the Quest for Humankind's
      Beginnings, by Virginia Morell (NY: Simon & Schuster, 1995).
By the Evidence: Memoirs, 1932-1951, by Louis Leakey (NY: Harcourt Brace
      Jovanovich, 1974).
Leakey's Luck: The Life of Louis Seymour Bazett Leakey, by Sonia Cole
      (NY: Harcourt Brace Jovanovich, 1975).
Walking with the Great Apes: Jane Goodall, Dian Fossey, Biruté Galdikas,
      by Sy Montgomery (Boston: Houghton Mifflin, 1991).
   . . . and many others, not to mention many magazine articles—those from
National Geographic are notable for their first-person accounts and great
photographs.

ACKNOWLEDGMENTS

Thanks to Maris, first and foremost.
Also: Tanya initially, Calista thoroughly,
Colleen graphically, Gina promotionally,
Mark editorially, and Kat, finally . . .
in all the best senses of the word.
—Jim Ottaviani

Thanks to Jim and all the folks at First Second (see above)
for making this happen. To Mum, for encouraging
my nerdy tendencies early on; Liz for the coffee;
Biggs for the purring; and Joe for, well . . . everything.
Lastly, thanks to everyone out there inspiring a
life-long love of all things art and science.
—Maris Wicks

JANE GOODALL, DIAN FOSSEY, and BIRUTÉ GALDIKAS
show us that knowledge brings compassion,
and compassion insists on action.
A portion of the author's proceeds will go to the following:

The Jane Goodall Institute
www.janegoodall.org

The Dian Fossey Gorilla Fund International
www.gorillafund.org

The Orangutan Foundation International
www.orangutan.org

First Second
New York

Text copyright © 2013 by Jim Ottaviani
Illustrations copyright © 2013 by Maris Wicks

Photo of Biruté Galdikas, Dian Fossey, and Jane Goodall on page 137 is used with permission from the Orangutan Foundation International (www.orangutan.org).

Published by First Second
First Second is an imprint of Roaring Brook Press,
a division of Holtzbrinck Publishing Holdings Limited Partnership
175 Fifth Avenue, New York, New York 10010

Design by Roberta Pressel

Cataloging-in-Publication Data is on file at the Library of Congress

ISBN: 978-1-59643-865-1

First Second books are available for special promotions and premiums.
For details, contact: Director of Special Markets, Holtzbrinck Publishers.

FIRST
EDITION
First Edition 2013

Printed in China by South China Printing Co. Ltd.,
Dongguan City, Guangdong Province

10 9 8 7 6 5 4 3 2